VULNERABLE

SEXUAL ABUSE AND PEOPLE WITH AN INTELLECTUAL HANDICAP

Y0-AGR-573

PREPARED BY
THE G. ALLAN ROEHER INSTITUTE
UNDER CONTRACT TO THE
FAMILY VIOLENCE PREVENTION
DIVISION, HEALTH AND
WELFARE CANADA

Canadian Cataloguing in Publication Data

Senn, Charlene Y., 1960 -
    Vulnerable: sexual abuse and people with an
intellectual handicap

Issued also in French under title: L'exploitation sexuelle et les personnes qui présentent une déficience intellectuelle.
ISBN 0-920121-32-2

1.   Sexually abused children.
2.   Mentally handicapped children.
3.   Mentally handicapped - Abuse of.
4.   Sex crimes.
I.   The G. Allan Roeher Institute.
II. Title

HQ71.S46 1988   362.7'044   C88-093704-1

The G. Allan Roeher Institute
York University, Kinsmen Building, 4700 Keele Street
Downsview, Ontario, M3J 1P3

Institute Director: Marcia H. Rioux
Project Director: Marcia H. Rioux
Publications Editor: Wanda Taylor
Desktop Publishing: Marion Brown
Researcher: Charlene Y. Senn

Canada's National Institute for the Study of Public Policy Affecting Persons with an Intellectual Impairment

The G. Allan Roeher Institute has two major goals:
- to identify and anticipate future trends that will support the presence, participation, self-determination and contribution of persons with an intellectual impairment in their communities;
- to foster the exchange of ideas leading to new ways of thinking about persons with an intellectual impairment.

The Institute conducts, sponsors and publishes research in a wide range of areas, with a major focus on public policy and funding, on studies of innovative social programs and on a the development of policy alternatives. It offers training programs and workshops across Canada on topics such as integrated education, employment, and alternatives to instrusives. Through its Information Services, which include a library, a book and film distribution service, and a computer accessible information system, The Institute provides up-to-date information to the public, professionals and community groups. The Institute also publishes the quarterly magazine **entourage.**

The G. Allan Roeher Institute is sponsored by the Canadian Association for Community Living, a voluntary organization bringing together over 400 local and twelve provincial and territorial associations working on behalf of persons with an intellectual impairment.

For more information about The G. Allan Roeher Institute, please contact us at:

4700 Keele Street, Kinsmen Building, York University, Downsview, Ont. M3J 1P3   (416) 661-9611

CONTENTS

Chapter 9

FOREWORD

Sexual abuse has become a major policy issue which all levels of government, education, industry, labour and services in Canada have been forced to address. Yet the sexual abuse of people with an intellectual handicap has figured as little more than a footnote in public discussion and policy-making.

Vulnerable shows how thoroughly the problem of sexual abuse and people with a mental handicap has been camouflaged — hidden away in institutions, rendered taboo elsewhere. Put away in institutions, denied opportunities for relationships, and denied a normal sex education, people with an intellectual handicap have been permitted to learn little about ordinary consequences and responsibilities. Denied their own sexuality, they tend to be uninformed on a fundamental aspect of their personal lives. And institutionalized for generations, they have been rendered fearfully vulnerable to sexual abuse. Is it any wonder that the relatively few sexual offences committed by individuals having an intellectual handicap have so frequently stemmed from the mystery surrounding their forbidden sexuality? *Vulnerable* teaches us that we can no longer deny that a problem exists.

If layers of denial and camouflage obscure the sexuality and abuse of people with an intellectual disability, this was not always the case. During "hysterical years" around the time of the First World War, the "feeble minded" were made to shoulder much of the burden for the criminality and sexual deviance which seemed to be undermining the already declining late-Victorian society. The menacing sexuality of the "feeble minded" was much talked about. These people would contaminate and dilute the race if left to breed unchecked, it was argued. It was vehemently urged to be a matter serious enough to warrant segregation, custodialism, sterilization and restrictive marriage laws. Governments accordingly entrenched the machinery of segregation and restriction. The supposed menace was banished or repressed. Those who were institutionalized were forced to lead obscure and controlled lives. The "putting away" therefore made it more possible for the unscrupulous to abuse without detection. While not an historical work, *Vulnerable* unmasks the current effects of a problem which has deep roots in history.

If we have long known that the "feeble minded" are not the sinister architects of society's moral offences, *Vulnerable* helps put that old bogey to rest, hopefully once and for all. Among other things it shows that in terms of national averages, people with an intellectual handicap are no more and no less guilty of sexual offences than are other citizens.

Besides looking at sexual abuse within the institutional setting, *Vulnerable* also looks at the problem in the community. It explores the systemic web of rejection and denial woven around sexual abuse survivors who have an intellectual handicap, a web which prevents them from benefitting from the systems and services set up for the rest of the population to deal with the problem. Once again, people with an intellectual handicap are seen to be shut out.

Vulnerable makes it impossible for us to escape the conclusion that people with an intellectual handicap must be seen as people above all — worthy of the same protections as other citizens against the criminal offences of others and worthy of being granted the same access to services as any other survivor of sexual abuse.

More than that, it calls into question the judicial system which treats adults with an intellectual handicap as children whose competency is in question. The courts have long held that age does not determine the competency of a witness. Yet still a judge holds the power to decide on a case-by-case basis whether a survivor of sexual abuse is credible when that survivor has an intellectual handicap. Often evidence is dismissed because of the individual's inability to communicate to the court by familiar means. This process is not good enough.

But *Vulnerable* shows that the issue of sexual abuse and people with an intellectual handicap is more than simply a legal problem. It is a problem caused by society's denial. Now is the time to bring the problem out of the dark and beyond the courtrooms into the residential facilities and sex education programs. Now is the time to provide or to extend existing services for abuse survivors to include people with an intellectual handicap, in recognition of their right to dignity, respect and support.

Up to now, the issue of sexual abuse and people with an intellectual handicap has not been treated in a comprehensive way in any research study. For the first time, *Vulnerable: Sexual Abuse and People with an Intellectual Handicap* uncovers the issues from all angles: prevalence of sexual abuse in people with an intellectual handicap; risk factors of developmental disability as related to sexual abuse; treatment and effects of abuse; accessibility of services; prevention; legal issues; and sex offenders who have an intellectual handicap.

We can only hope that this study will generate concrete action on behalf of sexual abuse survivors who have an intellectual handicap. Justice requires at least that much.

Marcia H. Rioux
Director, The G. Allan Roeher Institute
February, 1988
Toronto, Ontario

INTRODUCTION

Awareness of child sexual abuse in Canada was confined primarily to police stations and the offices of isolated doctors, psychiatrists, psychologists and child protection workers until the late 1970's. This is not surprising considering that the evolution of concern about child abuse in a country normally follows a "specific sequence of developmental stages" (Kempe, 1985, p. xxvii) with sexual abuse only being addressed at the fifth (or next to last) stage. According to Kempe, a society first recognizes and attempts to deal with the physical abuse of children and moves later to recognize the damage of physical neglect. Once this has been undertaken, cases of sexual abuse begin to appear in the caseloads of professionals previously unaware of the issue. But the occurrence of the sexual abuse of children is difficult for individuals to accept. The society is slow in addressing the issue because it also prefers to see the abuse as a rare and unfortunate circumstance. These beliefs are upheld by the society's structures which were not designed to meet the needs of children or to deal with sexual exploitation.

The legal system required corroboration for all testimony regarding sexual assault, inherent in which is the assumption of consent and the presumption of false claims. The psychiatric literature suggested that sexual abuse was the result of the odd demented offender (Lewis & Sarrell, 1969) or the seductive activity of pre-cocious children (Gager & Scheier, 1976) reinforcing the illusion of rarity. A "conspiracy of silence" (Butler, 1978) existed in the media whose reporters "chose" not to write about the cases of sexual abuse which came to their attention. Adult women who had experienced incest or abuse by a stranger when they were small, told no one of their experience and felt that they were alone. All of these pro-cesses, structural and individual served to preserve the illusion that child sexual abuse rarely occurred.

Due largely to the influence of the feminist movement, child sex-ual abuse (and more specifically incest,) became a public issue (e.g., Armstrong, 1979; Allen, 1980; Rush, 1980; Butler, 1978). Once the silence was broken, social workers, psychologists, public health nurses, physicians, and other professionals began to recognize how far-reaching the problem was. Political activism around missing children, the media's reporting of some sexual offences committed against children, and the publication of numerous volumes address-ing the problems and issues involving sexual abuse (Mayer, 1983; Whitcomb, 1982; Sgroi, 1982; Mrazek & Kempe, 1981), served to maintain the issue as one which required attention. Academics began conducting more in-depth research and publishing books and articles on their findings (Russell, 1984; Finkelhor, 1979; 1984; 1986) The helping professions responded by setting up treatment pro-grams and special child sexual abuse centres in major hospitals. Sex-ual abuse prevention programs began to be offered within the main-stream education system.

Once the community was reached by education or outreach efforts, the number of cases of sexual abuse coming forward over-whelmed the existing services. One study reported a 30,000 percent increase in reporting over seven years following community aware-ness of the issue (Giaretto, 1980 cited in Summit, 1983). Thus, the services are too few to address the needs of even a fraction of the cases which actually exist. Moreover, a bias occurs which means that those services which have been instituted help only particular types of children who have been abused. One of the most glaring gaps in the response to child sexual abuse has been the lack of discussion of the needs of "special populations" of children. Virtually all of the proposed and existing services have been aimed at the child who is able-bodied, hearing, sighted, and of average or greater intelligence.

This report will survey the literature which contributes to an understanding of the sexual abuse of children with developmental disabilities. It will be suggested that some children and adolescents with mental handicaps are at higher risk for sexual abuse than other children and adolescents. Further, an informal survey of existing programs and services suggests that the needs of children with mental handicaps are not being met either because they have not been recognized as a target population or because the service providers are so overwhelmed they have not welcomed the addition of another group of vulnerable individuals. General education of professionals and the public with regard to the sexual abuse of children with developmental disabilities needs to occur and discriminatory practices eliminated so these children can be afforded the rights and services available to other children. Further, the exclusion of children with intellectual impairments in the provision and planning of future services is a grave oversight which needs to be remedied immediately.

Definitional Issues

The definition of "mental retardation" utilized most commonly by researchers cited in this report is the one used by the American Association on Mental Deficiency and the American Psychiatric Associations Diagnostic and Statistical Manual of Mental Disorders (DSM-III). It comprises three features: (1) significantly sub-average general intellectual functions, (2) resulting in, or associated with, deficits or impairments in adaptive behavior, (3) with onset before the age of eighteen" (Aguilar, 1985, p.2). Problems arising from this type of definition have been summarized by Rioux (1979).

> First it is based on a combination of factors including a deficit in intellectual development and an impairment in social functioning ability and has a variety of causes. It does not fit therefore a strictly medical model or definition but rather is a social-administrative category. Secondly, the level of functioning disability varies significantly (from mild to profound). 'The gap in intelligence and functioning between the more profoundly mentally retarded and the mildly mentally retarded is greater than the gap between mildly mentally retarded and 'normal' persons.' (Friedman, 1976, p. 210) Thirdly, mental retardation is not a static condition, but is subject to change. That one of

the elements of mental retardation is a *deficit in adaptive behaviour* means that it is a product of the interaction between individual capacities and social demands. Changes in functioning ability or in the social demands made upon a person may result in a person no longer being classified as mentally retarded. The degree and nature of stimulation and education involved in the early nurturing process will have a direct correlation with the development of an individual. Therefore reliable assumptions made about individual potential cannot be made. Fourthly, it is a label or classification which is applied to a very diverse group of people (p. 17, emphasis in original).

For the purposes of this report the DSM-III definition will be used only as a general guideline for the boundaries of the population in question. A less offensive label will be used.

The terms "mental handicap", "intellectual handicap", "intellectual impairment", or "developmental disability" will be used in this report to refer to individuals who are disabled in some way by the condition described above. These terms are the ones preferred by activists and individuals with disabilities when they are required to provide a label (Park, 07/87; Worrell, 07/87; Richler, 07/97). It is stressed that "persons with developmental disabilities range widely in their development and abilities" (Blomberg, 1987, p. 9) therefore the label is used in this paper with respect for individual differences and the possibility/probability of developmental change.

The term child sexual abuse will be used in the widest possible sense here to mean any sexual use (contact or non-contact) or exploitation of a dependent person under the age of 16 as well as sexual exploitation and assault of individuals between the ages of 16 and 18. Both extrafamilial and intrafamilial abuse are included in this definition.

1

PREVALENCE OF CHILD SEXUAL ABUSE

In establishing the extent of a problem two estimates can be obtained, prevalence and incidence. While often used interchangeably these two estimates have considerably different meanings and are obtained with different degrees of difficulty. Prevalence estimates reveal generally how "widespread" the problem is or how "widely practiced" the behavior (Websters, 1969). In this general sense, any studies which give totals of the number of cases seen, the number of people reporting, et cetera, even without control groups, can contribute to prevalence estimates. In research terms, prevalence must be obtained by surveying a random sample of the adult population and assessing the percentage of them who have experienced the behavior or crime in question *in their lifetimes*. Incidence estimates on the other hand, are estimates of the "rate of occurrence" (Webster, 1969) of the abuse or victimization in the population. These estimates are usually given in terms of the number of cases per thousand individuals in *the given year* who have experienced the behavior, and are often based on reported cases. Thus the two are related but involve different aspects of an estimate of occurrence.

In the sexual abuse field, cases of abuse have been documented since the late seventies, however national prevalence studies have been conducted only more recently (Badgley et al., 1984; Russell, 1984; Finkelhor, 1984; Wyatt, 1985). Incidence studies may take as long as ten years to plan, carry out, analyze and write up for publication (Finkelhor & Associates, 1986). It is therefore not surprising that in a field as new as the study of sexual abuse of children with developmental disabilities, accurate estimates of prevalence and incidence have not yet been obtained. Our estimates of the frequency of sexual abuse in this population must therefore be derived from several sources. One standard source is the available prevalence studies with the recognition that they are often not well controlled or methodologically sound. Less common sources but ones which yield much information on the topic are legal documents, psychiatric reports, and sex education literature, which contain references to the sexual abuse of people with intellectual impairments.

Estimates from the 'normal' population

None of the existing studies of sexual abuse in the general population which have been published or carried out enable us to get an accurate estimate of the amount of sexual abuse suffered by children with intellectual impairments. This would not have occurred if the studies had included individuals with developmental disabilities in their random sample but they did not. Finkelhor and Associates (1986) have summarized the sampling techniques of all random sample studies. All of the techniques used to select samples would have excluded large numbers of adults with developmental disabilities through one means or another. Household selection (Badgley et al, 1984; Burnham, 1985, cited in Finkelhor & Assoc.; Miller, 1976) and telephone exchange selection (Bagley & Ramsay, 1986; Keckley Market Survey, 1983, cited in Finkelhor & Assoc., 1986; Lewis, 1985, cited in Finkelhor & Assoc.; Murphy, 1985, cited in Finkelhor & Assoc.; Russell, 1983; Wyatt, 1985) would only be accurate if people with developmental disabilities all had their own homes/ apartments and accompanying private telephones. Selection by driver's licenses (Kercher & McShane, 1984) or by parenting of children aged 6 to 14 (Finkelhor, 1984) would automatically exclude a large percentage of adults who are disabled. The length of the questionnaires administered would likely rule out the few adults with intellectual impairments who were reached, commonly being one to one and a half hours in length. It is obvious that other groups of people such as those who are hearing impaired, blind, physically or mentally disabled may also not be part of such "random" sampling procedures unless researchers make a concerted effort to reach them.

How do we know that children with developmental disabilities are sexually abused?

Long before any attempts were made to document the sexual abuse of individuals with a mental handicap empirically, assumptions that these children and adolescents were vulnerable to exploitation were common. In the legal documentations required for the request for sterilization of a severely disabled young girl, the likelihood of pregnancy due to "the constant threat of being assaulted and ravished" (p. 469) was listed as a reason for the request (M.K.R., 1974). A summary of several such cases was given as follows: "The inconvenience of caring for the incompetent child coupled with fear of sexual promiscuity or exploitation may lead parents to seek a solution which infringes their offspring's fundamental procreative rights" (A.W., 1981, p. 370).[1] Two cases of incest were reported to have been discovered by doctors performing pre-sterilization evaluations (Perrin et al, 1976). A geneticist's study of the offspring of incestuous relationships revealed that over 14 percent of the women who bore children by their fathers or brothers were classified as "mentally subnormal". Besides documenting the existence of incest, this figure is much higher than that which would be expected by chance alone.

Documentation from juvenile homes and institutions show that young adolescents considered to be "mentally retarded" were considered prime targets for exploitation and were often incarcerated for "their own protection" (Wooden, 1976; Rogers, 1972).[2] In addition, the literature on sex education with children and adolescents with intellectual impairments frequently mentions the concern of parents of disabled children and workers in homes and institutions that the children are particularly vulnerable to exploitation (Fischer & Krajicek, 1974; Simonds, 1980; Bennett, Vockell & Vockell, 1972; Goodman, 1973). While some parental fears are likely unfounded, the anecdotal data found in other sources suggests that some of the fears are based on estimates of their child's vulnerability and knowledge of other cases of abuse.

Anecdotal evidence, case histories, and assumptions hidden in related texts, all show that sexual abuse of children with developmental disabilities is a problem. What they cannot provide is the more detailed information about the extent of the problem.

Extent of the Problem

The studies which will now be presented are the only ones which have specifically addressed the issue of sexual abuse of children with developmental disabilities. Some have uncovered the information as a result of a study of another population. Others planned to address this topic from the outset. Regardless, all of the studies have some methodological or sampling problems which make their findings less generalizable than they might be. Therefore they are utilized here to suggest the extent of the problem rather than to confirm it.

Chamberlain et al. (1984) interviewed 69 adolescent girls with developmental disabilities in contact with the Cincinatti Adolescent Clinic. The girls sampled represented 70 percent of the group originally contacted and no difference was found between interviewed and non-interviewed girls on the basis of demographic characteristics. Subjects ranged in age from 11 to 23 years. The subjects also ranged in terms of their disability with "a lower distribution of IQs than would be expected in a random sample" (p. 446). Twenty-two (25%) of the girls had experienced rape or attempted rape. Of these, seven were sexually assaulted by a father, stepfather, or foster father; three were assaulted by another family member. At least two victims were sexually assaulted while at school; one perpetrator was known to be the girl's teacher. In other words, the majority of perpetrators were known to the victims. The average age at the time of the assault was 14 with a range from 9 to 17 years old, thus all represented child sexual abuse. Chamberlain et al. (1984) stressed that one-third of the "mildly retarded" girls had been sexually assaulted suggesting that they may be at higher risk. It must also be noted that only rape and attempted rape were included in the definition of sexual assault, therefore these figures likely underestimate the extent of the problem.

Ryerson (1984) has reported the results of a seven-year study conducted by Seattle Rape Relief. During the seven-year period from 1977 to 1983, 700 cases of sexual abuse were reported involving children and adults with intellectual impairments. While some of these case were sexual assaults of adult women and men, "case

reviews indicate that victimization often begins with children between two and five years of age and continues for a period of five to
15 years" (p. 6). Moreover, 99 percent of the victims with developmental disabilities were abused by a relative or caretaker.

Cowardin (1987) has taken the Seattle Rape Relief figures for one
year (1980) and by comparing the figures with California's known
reported rapes, found that people with intellectual impairments in
King County reported sexual assault at four times the national rate.
(See Table 1) This is even higher when it is estimated that only 20
percent of assaults are reported by victims with developmental disabilities (Ryerson, 1984).

Hard (1986) conducted a study of the case records of 95 adults
with developmental disabilities enrolled at a work activity centre.
She then interviewed 65 of the individuals using a questionnaire she
developed to obtain more detailed information. Hard (1986) reported
that 83 percent of the women and 32 percent of the men had experienced prior sexual abuse. The ages of the subjects of this study
ranged from 17-48 years. Of the 38 individuals for which age at the
time of abuse was available, 17 or 45 percent were under 18 years of
age when the abuse happened. Again, 99 percent of the victims were
assaulted by a perpetrator known to them. Although the results are
generalizable only to people involved in work activity centers,
Hard's research is probably the best estimate we have at the current
time on the prevalence of sexual assault and abuse in the population
with developmental disabilities. Another important point is that 30
individuals were not interviewed even though their files were originally selected. Reasons for this were that "several were non-verbal,
a few chose not to be interviewed, two did not understand the
questions, and others had left the . . . program prior to the interview" (p. 1).

Studies which document sexual abuse against institutionalized or
foster-parented children provide some evidence for this type of
abuse against mentally handicapped children in these settings even
though their subject populations were not so restricted. Musick
(1984) interviewed a select sample of former mental patients who
had been victimized as well as staff in mental institutions who had
been aware of sexual abuse of patients. While the study focussed on
mental institutions rather than institutions which house predom-
inantly individuals with developmental disabilities, Musick's
conclusions about the factors which make inmates/patients/clients
vulnerable would have parallels in other institutionalized

populations. She suggests that structural factors and treatment practices such as "staffing practices which allow male staff to care for and escort women patients, inadequate supervision and control of male patients in gender-integrated spaces, inadequate supervision of heavily medicated, restrained, or isolated female patients . . ." (p. 2) make individuals in the institution particularly vulnerable.

Dawson (undated) conducted a survey of Ontario Children's Aid Societies and the Central Child Abuse Register in an attempt to assess the extent of abuse in foster-care services between 1979 and 1981. Twenty agencies out of the 51 which had been contacted participated in the study. The data which he reports on the occurrence of sexual abuse are startling. Forty-two percent of Aid Societies cases and 38 percent of the cases on the register which involved foster parents were incidents of sexual abuse. Foster fathers were the perpetrators in all cases. Girls between the ages of 13 and 17 were the most common victims although victims were as young as four years old. Two boys were also victimized. Dawson (undated) reported that 60 percent of the children who had been abused had been identified as having special needs; 17 percent of these were classified as having a moderate mental handicap. While it is not possible to tell whether the children with developmental disabilities were sexually victimized, it is clear from this and other data (e.g., Chamberlain et al., 1984) that some children in foster care are sexually abused by their foster fathers.

Sampling Difficulties.

A random sample study of individuals with developmental disabilities would be difficult to carry out and likely unproductive. People with developmental disabilities live in institutions (less than 10%), and they live in foster homes; they live in group homes and they live independently; many children live with their families of origin. They vary in their functioning level from those needing complete care (toileting, feeding, etc.) to those who are completely functioning in the community. Most people with developmental disabilities are nearer to the "complete functioning" end of the continuum with 75 to 90 percent of them having borderline or mild impairment "without significant organic handicap" (Szymanski, 1977, p. 68). This means that many of those individuals one wanted to study would not be reached by surveying only special facilities. Studies which attempt to accurately estimate abuse of people with developmental disabilities must sample across these situations.

A paradox has occurred in research involving the sexuality of people with intellectual impairments. Many of the studies establishing a need for sex education of people with a mental handicap have focussed at least partially on the institutional setting (Edmonson & Wish, 1975; Coleman & Murphy, 1980; Hall, Morris & Barker, 1973; Hall & Morris, 1976; Edmonson, McCombs & Wish, 1979) assuming that sexual exploitation is a reality in that setting. Yet no published studies have been able to access institutions to document evidence of sexual abuse. The exclusion of people in institutional or full-care settings may cause underestimation of the problem as there are theoretical reasons to suggest that individuals in "complete care" may be extremely vulnerable to the whims of caretakers. In these circumstances the living situation is confounded also by the degree of handicap which the person has, although this is not always the case. Some researchers recognize the vulnerability of the more severely disabled institutionalized people but are prevented by circumstances from surveying them (Musick, 1987; Hard, 1987). The difficulty in obtaining access to institutions has been stressed by these researchers. This is also supported by other people in the field who are not researchers. Davies (05/87) suggested that she is only called into institutions/group homes to do prevention workshops once there has already been a problem with abuse, however she is still not informed that it has occurred.[3] While it is understandable that institutions would not want to open themselves up to legal suits and public outrage purposefully, the refusal to entertain research could be construed as negligence.

Another problem is that research has not been able to adequately assess the vulnerability of people with the most severe disabilities. This will continue unless creative ways are found to lower existing communication barriers. Cases of abuse of people with limited verbal skills currently will only come to light if medical symptoms of sexual abuse (e.g., pregnancy, venereal disease) *are* present and diagnosed, if the abuse is witnessed (by another client or worker) *and* reported, or if the individual is somehow able to indicate that the abuse has occurred verbally or nonverbally.

Surveying a random sample of people with developmental disabilities would be extremely difficult. Research which would best assess the extent of the problem would likely occur by sampling across the different types of settings in which people with intellectual

impairments live and by attempting to survey a sample of individuals with the widest range of disabilities that is feasible. Musick
(05/87) has suggested that simple access to the medical records of
the residents in institutions would give a researcher of sexual abuse
a section of the population that has not yet been identified. Until the
time that more creative research has been conducted it must be
recognized that only a fraction of the picture has yet been
uncovered.

2

DEVELOPMENTAL DISABILITIES
AS A RISK FACTOR

It is apparent that sexual abuse of children with developmental disabilities is occurring. It is important to understand the role that the disability plays in their victimization. The likelihood of a child with a developmental disability being sexually abused is dependent upon whether the presence of the disability has a protective function, has no effect, or puts the child at higher risk of abuse. If the disability has a protective function then the child's probability of being victimized would be lower than children in the 'normal' population. If the disability acts as a risk factor, a higher percentage of children with developmental disabilities would be sexually abused than would be predicted in the 'normal' population. If the presence of a developmental disability is not related to sexual abuse then children with intellectual impairments would be at an equal risk for abuse as other children.

There is very little support for the suggestion that the presence of a mental handicap protects children against abuse. The belief that individuals will feel sorry for or are protective of children with handicaps and therefore would not consider them as potential targets for abuse is documented by several authors (Watson, 1984; Minnesota Dept. of Corrections, 1983; Cole, 1986; Worthington, 1984). This does not seem likely. In the case of physical abuse, much has been written to suggest that differently abled children are at higher risk for abuse. Rationales given for this relationship vary; some researchers believe that the stresses of parenting a handicapped child contribute to parent's abusive behavior (Helfer, 1975; Sandgrund et al, 1974; Barth & Blythe, 1983; Glaser & Bentovim, 1979), some suggest that parents have unrealistic expectations of their "borderline" children who appear "normal" but are actually disabled in some way (Morse, Sahler & Friedman, 1970; Souther, undated) or that it is a combination of these factors (Friedrich & Boriskin, 1978; Solomons, 1979; Gil, 1970). Other researchers suggest that the relationship exists due to a causal link in the other direction, that is, many forms of child abuse involve head and brain trauma which in turn causes impaired intellectual functioning (Diamond & Judes, 1983; Elmer & Gregg, 1967; Caffey, 1974; Appelbaum, 1980) or that abuse is paired with neglect, poverty, and poor nutrition, which are related to decreased intellectual potential (Starr, Dietrich, Fischoff, Ceresnie & Zweier, 1984). The consensus among these authors is that whatever the basis for the relationship, there does seem to be a higher risk for children with a developmental disability to be physically abused. (See Martin, Beezley, Conway & Kempe, 1974; Alexander, 1979 for a comprehensive review of this literature.) While no research documents the relationship between sexual child abuse and developmental disabilities empirically, many of the aforementioned studies included sexual abuse in their definition of abuse. Also it has been noted that "While sexual molestation is rarely commented on in reports of battered children (usually infants and very young children), it may be assumed that the probability of sexual abuse at an older age is increased in a family in which violence and physical assault are present." (Martin et al, 1974, p. 40) Thus, without evidence that a mental handicap protects children from being sexually abused it must be assumed that children with intellectual impairments are at least at as great a risk as other children.

According to the most recent national prevalence study, research conducted for the Badgley report, this would mean that at least 39 percent of girls and 16 percent of boys with developmental disabilities will be sexually abused[4] before the age of 18.

There is considerable evidence accumulated to suggest that children and adolescents with developmental disabilities are in fact at higher risk for sexual abuse. It has been documented by some authors (e.g., Shuker, 1980 cited in Longo & Gochenour, 1981) that some incarcerated sex offenders report selecting their victims on the basis of perceived vulnerability. A major men's magazine once instructed its readers that "mentally retarded" girls were ideal targets for sexual abuse as they would not be able to identify their attacker (Hustler cited in Sank & LaFleche, 1981). Elaboration of the concept of increased vulnerability will occur later.

Thus, when national prevalence studies are combined with those studies which specifically studied people with developmental disabilities, it must be estimated that between 39 (Badgley et al, 1984) and 68 percent (Hard, 1986) of girls with developmental disabilities and between 16 (Badgley et al., 1984) and 30 percent (Hard, 1986) of boys with developmental disabilities will be subjected to sexual abuse before they reach 18 years of age. These figures are staggering even at their lowest and clearly indicate the need for prevention and intervention strategies.

How does the disability act as a risk factor?

With such a large proportion of children predicted to be victims of sexual abuse it is important to assess the reasons for this vulnerability to be able to guide prevention and intervention efforts.

Finkelhor (1984; 1986) put forward a theory of sexual abuse which asserts that four preconditions are necessary before any sexual abuse of children can occur. First, the adult must be predisposed to abuse. Second, internal inhibitions against abusing must be reduced. Third, external (social) restraints must be reduced, and finally, the child's own restraints and protections must be overcome. The fact of a child's disability would likely be involved only in the last three stages of this model with emphasis on the last two stages. The abuse of any child requires a perpetrator with the desire to sexually abuse a child.

This four factor model has been expanded by Russell (1987) to include ways in which these preconditions could be created in our society. (See Figure 1) An examination of this elaboration is useful in attempting to explain the increased vulnerability of children with intellectual impairments. Only those features of the model which are thought to be differentially invoked for children with developmental disabilities and those without will be mentioned. All others are assumed to be in effect to a greater or lesser extent based on other circumstances. It will be seen that the fact of the child's disability may serve to reinforce the perpetrators own beliefs and help to excuse or justify the assault. In addition, from the perspective of the child victim, her[5] disability may indirectly place her in a situation in which she is physically or emotionally more vulnerable to assault.

The reduction of the perpetrator's internal inhibitions can be facilitated by a number of beliefs held in society about children and sexual relations with them. These beliefs would be exacerbated by myths held in society about people with mental handicaps. For example, the rationalizations of some adults that little harm is done to a child in sexual activity could be stretched further if the adult believed that the child with an intellectual impairment "would not know what was happening" (Burgess, Groth, Holmstrom & Sgroi, 1978) or that it wouldn't affect them anyway (Women Against Rape, undated). In addition, just as the view of women and children as commodities may justify their exploitation (Rush, 1980), persons with developmental disabilities are considered by some to be subhuman (Morgenstern, 1973), and thus worth less than other women and children. The process of dehumanization in which the person is made into an object or something less than fully human would reduce inhibitions against aggressing against them.

Reduction of social inhibitions can be achieved by attitudinal or situational means. Pornography which advocates the abuse of girls with Down syndrome because no one will believe them (Hustler) portrays little empathy for the child victim and could have an effect on attitudes about the child with a developmental disability either by creating or reinforcing negative stereotypes. The power disparity between adults and children which may reduce inhibitions against acting sexually with a child is even further exaggerated in the case of children who are emotionally deprived or dependent on adults. While so called normal children have a limited number of adults upon whom they are dependent (teachers, parents) the child with a developmental disability may, through the provision of extra care and services, be exposed to many more adults who are in control of them (Watson, 1984; Murphy & Della Corte, 1987; Hyman, 07/87). By chance alone, the increased number of adult care givers may increase the likelihood of one of them being an abuser. In addition, dependency on adult figures may be encouraged more in children with intellectual impairments (Watson, 1984). A compliant dependent child is easier to take care of than a rebellious independent one. As Butler (1980) points out, good children make good victims.

Finkelhor and associates (1986) have compiled the most comprehensive profile of risk factors associated with the child based on a thorough review of the literature of both incest and extrafamilial abuse (see Figure 2). It must be noted that none of the studies from which these risk factors were derived, had subjects with intellectual impairments. The assumption is being made that the factors which are found to make 'normal' children more vulnerable to abuse will apply equally to children with developmental disabilities. Moreover, it is asserted that the fact that a child has a developmental disability will in many cases put that child at higher risk for abuse for reasons which are only indirectly related to their intellectual capacity.

1. Child is emotionally deprived. Emotional deprivation could potentially occur by separating a child from her/his family, not providing a nurturant or stimulating environment, or preventing a child from making friends or contacts outside the family. The removal of children with developmental disabilities from their families of origin because supportive services are not available, and placing them in foster homes, group homes, or institutions, could in some instances create a situation in which a child is emotionally deprived. On the other hand, some families may not be able to cope with a "special" child and may create an environment in their own home in which the child is not provided with adequate stimulation and care. It has already been established that children with intellectual impairments appear to be at higher risk for physical abuse and neglect in their own homes than other children (Martin, Beezley, Conway & Kempe, 1974; Alexander, 1979). Thus, one could argue that the probability of a child with an intellectual impairment being removed from her/his home is higher than for a child who does not have a disability. Szymanski and Jansen (1980) suggest that some children who have developmental disabilities may have an increased need for affection which may be harder for parents to meet. Cole (1986) characterises the families of children with intellectual impairments as tending to be either affectionally depriving or overloading. These behaviors might create increased vulnerability in the child.

2. Child is socially isolated. This risk factor was originally conceptualized to involve strictly geographic isolation with children in rural settings usually being found to be at higher risk than those in urban environments (Summit & Kryso, 1978; Finkelhor, 1984; Russell, 1986). Finkelhor (1979; 1986) has suggested that the concept of social isolation should be used in the broadest possible sense, including isolation from peers, isolation "caused by poverty, family constellation, shyness, or unusual value systems" (1979, p. 149). The family with a child with a developmental disability may not be able to access the support systems which are necessary for them to cope with the situation. In other cases, the family may be cut off from everyone except the professionals who are paid to respond to them. Both of these situations are isolating and may put their child(ren) at higher risk.

3 & 4. Child knows adult and has special fondness for adult. Virtually all children are warned about strangers, few are told about the risk of abuse by someone they know and trust (Summit, 1983). The reality is that children are more likely to be sexually assaulted by someone they know (Finkelhor, 1979; 1986; Russell, 1984; Conte & Berliner, 1981). The data reviewed earlier examining the abuse of children with intellectual impairments, suggests that they are even more likely to be sexually molested by a relative or caretaker (Hard, 1986; Ryerson, 1984). More children with developmental disabilities are dependent on adults for personal care for a longer time period (Varley, 1984), and more children with developmental disabilities receive special services which are given by a trusted adult (for example, bus drivers, special education teachers, and staff in residential programs) than other children (Watson, 1984; Baladerian, undated; Murphy & Della Corte, 1987). Thus, the child who has a disability might be more vulnerable to abuse from a known adult. In the case of more severe disability, authors have mentioned that the child may have the fear that she will not get the care necessary for her survival if she protests or reports the abuse (PACER, 1986).[6] Due to the integral role that many of these adults play in the child's life, the child is likely to form a strong emotional attachment with them. While this is a positive situation in most cases, the greater number of caregivers and increased dependency on them could contribute to the increased vulnerability of the child with the developmental disability.

5. Child is vulnerable to incentives offered by adult. Many children are vulnerable to abuse because they desire the objects, food, or other rewards the perpetrator offers them. Children who are poor, are deprived, have been institutionalized with few belongings, or who have few freedoms, are probably more vulnerable to these incentives. An example of this was found in an old study of sexuality in an institutional setting which mentioned as an aside that some adolescent girls had performed sexual favors for groups of boys in the facility simply because they wanted rewards they were offered (Edgerton & Dingman, 1964; Mitchell, 1985). While many children are taught not to accept candy or presents from strangers (which will not prevent them from accepting them from a known adult) this small scale "protection" strategy is not necessarily taught to children with developmental disabilities. As will be seen later when prevention is addressed, most children with intellectual impairments are not prepared to protect themselves in even the most minor ways. Thus, there is the possibility that they could be more open to bribery by adults. This is complicated by the difficulty children with developmental disabilities may have in recognizing tricks adults are using to manipulate them (PACER, 1986; Watson, 1984; Baladerian, undated).

6. **Child feels helpless and powerless.** Children with developmental disabilities have been "particularly trained to be obedient, polite, 'nice to adults' and (to) do what they are told" (Baladerian, undated, p. 3). The situation of extreme dependency on adults and the expectancy of failure in children with intellectual impairments has been postulated to create learned helplessness (Vigilanti, undated). Sometimes, their parents have been overprotective so they lack a sense of empowerment which other children possess (PACER, 1986). In addition, a lack of peer relationships may prevent the development of healthy self-esteem (Moglia, 1986). Any or all of these factors could serve to make the child with a disability who has been taught that he or she is different and in need of protection more likely to feel powerless.

7. **Child is ignorant of what is happening.** Children's lack of adequate information about their bodies and sexuality has been related to increased risk of sexual abuse for several years. Virtually all of the prevention programs have an informational component along these lines. In the case of children with developmental disabilities some authors have pointed out that parents and other caretakers may deny their children's sexuality (Moglia, 1986; Rose, 1986; Forchuk, Pitkeathly, Cook, Allen & St. Denis McDonald, 1984; Goodman, 1973) and that they have little or no access to sex education (Hard, 1986; Blomberg, 1986; Sengstock & Vergason, 1970). Thus, this is one area in which children with developmental disabilities are particularly vulnerable. If they do not understand what is happening to them, it is unlikely that they would know that they could say no. Furthermore, if they are not adequately informed about their bodies, they would have difficulty being understood if they tried to tell someone once the abuse had occurred.

8. **Child is sexually repressed and has sexual curiosity.** All of the factors mentioned under 7 above have the additional effect of creating

an environment in which healthy sexual curiosity and discovery are not encouraged. This is even more obvious in many institutional settings in which consensual sexual activity (including kissing) is punished or discouraged (Coleman & Murphy, 1980). "Thus, retarded adolescents have little opportunity to satisfy their sexual curiosity and urges, which otherwise may be normal. As a result, they may become easy victims of sexual exploitation and abuse." (Szymanski & Jansen, 1980).

   9. Coercion. There is no evidence that children with intellectual impairments are at greater risk for coercion than other children. It may be easier however for the perpetrator to use coercive tactics such as tricking, manipulating, bribing, scaring, or threatening the child with a developmental disability to comply. It is important to stress that sexual abuse of a child need not be accompanied by physical force to be effected.

   In the case of physical child abuse it appears to be factors directly related to the handicapping condition which are in some way responsible for the abuse such as, stress in parenting (e.g., Sandgrund et al., 1974) or unrealistic expectations (Morse, Sahler, & Friedman, 1970). In the situation of sexual abuse it does not seem to be the actual disability which creates the vulnerability but rather the training received, the type of education (or lack thereof), and the environment in which children with developmental disabilities find themselves, that puts them at higher risk for sexual abuse. In other words, society has created a situation in which children with developmental disabilities have been taught to be "good victims".

3

IDENTIFICATION OF
CHILD SEXUAL ABUSE

"Recognition of sexual molestation of a child is entirely dependent on the individual's inherent willingness to entertain the possibility that the condition may exist." (Sgroi, 1975, p. 20 cited in Summit, 1983, p. 116). This observation by Sgroi (1975) was and unfortunately still is in many cases an accurate representation of the situation within the medical and other professions. Today, as people are beginning to address the sexual abuse of children with disabilities, a similar reaction is likely to occur. Just as Freud could not admit to himself that the sexual abuse of daughters by fathers was widespread (Rush, 1980; 1983), many people do not want to accept or believe that children who are disabled are victimized (Cole, 1986). Moreover, myths about the sexuality of disabled people create an atmosphere in which denial of the problem is more likely.

Myths about people with mental handicaps abound. For some people, they are sexless entities, and will remain asexual and child-like all their lives (Rose, 1986; Szymanski, 1977; Cole, 1986). Compounded by the sexist myths that sexual abuse is about sex, that people with developmental disabilities are not sexually attractive, and that perpetrators would therefore not consider them likely targets (WAR, undated) these myths create an environment in which people experience disbelief that anyone would sexually use a child with an intellectual impairment. Paradoxically myths also exist which suggest that people with developmental disabilities are "over-sexed and unable to inhibit sexual impulses" (Szymanski, 1977, p. 113-114). It should be noted that this was one of the arguments of choice for individuals and groups in the eugenics movement for the sterilization of all people labelled mentally retarded (Rioux, 1979). While this belief has been applied mostly to adults, it is conceivable that some people would consider it to be true of children as well. As mentioned earlier, the myth of the seductive child exists in the sexual abuse literature, particularly in the psychoanalytic research. There is no reason to expect that these authors would not apply the same logic (or lack thereof) to children with developmental disabilities. One example of the myth of the seductive child was even found in a volume addressing the counselling needs of special populations including those with developmental disabilities (Johnson & Kempton, 1981).

It is crucial that parents, professionals and other helpers come to the realization that child sexual abuse occurs because children are powerless to resist and that all children are powerless to a greater or lesser degree. Therefore sexual abuse must be viewed as a possibility whenever the child's symptoms or verbalizations point to it.

Symptoms of child sexual abuse

There are many ways sexual abuse may be detected, ranging from the most obvious, in which an adult witnesses a child being abused, to the most subtle behavioral changes. Each of these will be discussed with emphasis on detection of abuse of children with developmental disabilities.[7]

Discovery of abuse. Burgess & Holmstrom (1978) discuss the possibility in some cases that the sexual abuse is witnessed by a parent or other person. While this appears to be fairly rare, for example, as the result of an unexpected arrival by an adult, the situation may be more common in the case of sexual abuse in institutions. Duffett (06/87) reported in a conversation with the author that some women with developmental disabilities who had come in contact with the rape crisis center reported having witnessed the sexual abuse of other people in their institutions. It seems that in this setting the perpetrator was not concerned about witnesses, assured that no one would believe them. While the rationale is conjecture (this type of occurrence is not reported or explained in the literature), it is something which should be investigated. If these witnesses were believed and were considered competent to testify, the perpetrator's lack of care would make a prosecutor's case much easier.

Verbal Disclosures. The next most obvious clue that sexual abuse has occurred (besides witnessing it) is a child's verbal report that someone has touched them or made them touch the adult, in a sexual manner. However, it must be remembered that verbal disclosures are possible only for some children. Mian et al. (1986) reported that one third of the cases of sexual abuse which were brought to a Toronto hospital involved children under 6 years old. Very young children may not have adequate verbal skills to disclose the abuse. Furthermore, only a minority of verbal children tell anyone explicitly about the abuse, particularly when it first occurs (Finkelhor, 1979; Burgess & Holmstrom, 1978). Secrecy is a crucial part of the dynamics of child sexual abuse (Summit, 1983; Burgess & Holmstrom, 1978; Sgroi, 1982). The perpetrator usually threatens the child either with physical harm or with dire consequences to the child and the child's family if the "secret" is divulged (Rose, 1986; Sgroi, 1982; Summit, 1983). Examples of the extreme threats to children abound in the literature and it is quite clear why most children do not tell. Most children are taught to listen to adults and they believe the threats no matter how far fetched they seem to adults. Developmentally disabled children may be even more susceptible to tricks, bribes and threats than other children (Watson, 1984).

The form that most disclosures of sexual abuse take keep many adults from accepting the information. Summit (1983) has devoted much of his writing to an explanation of this phenomenon. In his estimation, adults impose their own expectations of the way a child "should" react, (e.g., should tell immediately, should fight back) and these are based on misconceptions. The child, on the other hand, has been put under tremendous pressure not to disclose under any circumstances. When disclosure does occur then it is most often "delayed", that is, following long after the incident(s), or "conflicted" and/or "unconvincing", for example coming at a time which the adult feels is entirely inappropriate or out of context. To further complicate this situation, even if the child is believed and action taken, the "normal" progression in the child's psychological progression through the trauma, is for the child to retract the disclosure once she realizes the devastation in her own and others' lives which has occurred as a result of it (Summit, 1983). Hyman (17/07/87) believes that children with intellectual impairments may be even more likely to recant and say that the abuse never happened. They may have increased fear of living away from their families. They may be intimidated by their families attempts to discredit them. Whatever the reason, Hyman stresses that recanting is a normal part of the process following sexual abuse.

The disclosures of children and adolescents with developmental disabilities have not been studied by researchers or been well documented by clinicians as yet. Observations from people working in the prevention field who work with children and adolescents with developmental disabilities are therefore the only source of information. It has been suggested that the disclosures individuals with developmental disabilities make may appear strange to people who are not knowledgeable or prepared. In Anderson's (06/87) experience adolescents may disclose their abuse in graphic detail in front of a group of people while showing little emotion. Duffet (05/87) supports this observation but feels that it may be confounded by the fact that many of the adolescents and adults in these groups were on various medications which are known to have effects on their emotional state. The observations do support the assertion that there are wide individual differences between people in the way they report abuse. Emphasis is placed on the suggestion that adults listen to disclosures from children and adolescents and respond to the child's needs rather than trying to impose on them how they "should" react.

There are no accurate estimates of the percentage of cases of child sexual abuse in which the child does tell someone directly although retrospective studies like those of Finkelhor (1979) and Russell (1984) indicate that very few cases (less than 5%) are reported to the police. There also appears to be a screening process by which disclosure of intrafamilial abuse rarely gets reported to police while extra-familial abuse is reported more commonly (Russell, 1983).

There are also no accurate estimates of the number of disclosures made to family members or the police by children and adolescents with intellectual impairments. The best estimate available is from Hard's (1986) study of adults in a work activity center. In this study, 64 percent of the females and 40 percent of the males who had been sexually abused told someone. While not all of these experiences happened when the person was a child, the figures are interesting. Not surprisingly, in all of the cases of sexual abuse in which the victim did *not* tell, the perpetrator was a member of the family (Hard, 1986).

Non-verbal Disclosures. Burgess & Homstrom (1983) suggest that while many children do not or cannot tell anyone about the abuse, some children are able to communicate non-verbally its occurrence. Examples are given such as a child coming home without clothes, disappearing overnight or becoming pregnant at a very young age. Less obvious but still meaningful clues are the results of bribery, such as the accumulation of money or candy. Children who are afraid to tell but wish to disclose, may draw or paint pictures which incorporate their representations of the abuse to try to attract attention to their situation (Burgess & Holmstrom, 1978). It is not known how often these clues are given by children and of those how many are unrecognized or misunderstood.

Masked signs and symptoms. Many authors have published lists of signs and symptoms which are connected with child sexual abuse (Minnesota Dept. of Corrections, 1983; Conte, 1986; Watson, 1984; Murphy & Della Corte, 1987). These "symptoms will vary with the child's age, the nature of the trauma, and the ego strengths of the child" (Price & Valdiserri, 1981, p. 232). Some of the signs and symptoms have been found by medical and psychological investigation of children who have disclosed sexual abuse. Others, which are referred to as "masked" cases, were identified when a symptom was presented for treatment by a child or parent and upon further investigation sexual abuse was found to be the origin.

Physical signs and symptoms. Some of the symptoms on these lists are strictly physical such as, "genital infections or soreness" (Minnesota Dept. of Corrections, 1983, p. 4), "vaginal or penile discharge", "bruises or bleeding in the genital or anal areas" (Watson, 1984, p. 18), "difficulty in walking", "torn, stained, or bloody underclothing" (Murphy & Della Corte, 1987, p. 2), and pregnancy (Sgroi, 1982). It is clear that these symptoms are fairly straightforward and always require a quick response usually with medical intervention. This response is warranted even if abuse is not the cause.

Hunter, Kilstrom, and Loda (1985) report that "genital symptoms" were the most common "masked" symptoms. They were present in 36 percent of the masked cases. Another study of children brought to a hospital because of suspected or known sexual abuse reported that 16 percent of the children were found to have genital trauma and 24 percent had signs of infection (Rimisza &

Niggemann, 1982). They also point out that six patients were brought to the clinic because of "symptoms of infection" and sexual abuse was subsequently discovered.

Not all children who have been sexually abused exhibit these types of physical trauma as a result of their abuse (Price & Valdiserri, 1981). In a Canadian study, Mian et al. (1986) found that 24 percent of the children under six had physical symptoms only, while 12 percent had physical symptoms combined with other types of symptoms at the time of disclosure. Almost two-thirds of the children had no physical symptoms. Research on sexual abuse of boys suggests that they are somewhat more likely to experience physical injury (Ellerstein & Canavan, 1980) however this has not yet been substantiated in other studies.

Non-genital physical symptoms. Burgess & Holmstrom (1978) present a case illustration of an 11-year-old girl admitted to hospital with sharp stomach pains. Once admitted the pains, vomiting and diarrhea cease. When questioned by her mother she revealed that she had been raped four times by her father. Hunter, Kilstrom and Loda (1985) support this case with the finding that 12 percent of masked sexual abuse cases were presented at the hospital with "psychosomatic" abdominal pain. This kind of data makes it clear that focus on genital injuries as the "proof" of sexual abuse would be erroneous.

The detection of sexual abuse from physical symptoms depends upon the knowledge of the adult with whom the child comes in contact. Most children without disabilities would be taken to a family doctor, clinic, or hospital when they exhibited pain or other explicit symptoms. Children in institutions and many children in group homes do not use standard medical facilities. Rather, a doctor visits the facility. Unfortunately, this policy may result in a less vigorous investigation of the symptoms (for example, hospitals often use a sexual abuse team of specialists). In addition, whereas the child brought to the hospital would be in contact with many people, one of whom hopefully has the training to detect sexual abuse, the institutionalized child is forced to rely on the expertise (or lack thereof) of one physician. This is a serious problem which must be addressed.

Behavioral symptoms. Behavioral symptoms are probably the most frequent. The research does not reflect this. Behavioral signs may remain unnoticed by parents in the absence of other symptoms. Even if the behavioral signs were noticed, it is unlikely that they would be brought to the attention of the medical profession. The best list of these behavioral indicators is provided by Sgroi (1982) which is reproduced in Figure 3. Parents and professionals sometimes become confused when confronted with lists of this type as many of the symptoms could be the result of other traumas or part of a normal "phase" in a child's development. Sgroi (1982) stresses that while these symptoms are suggestive of abuse they are not in themselves proof of abuse. Berliner (02/85) pointed out that people should look for constellations of symptoms, clusters of signs, or changes from the child's normal behavior. Conte (1986) suggests that the symptom lists should be used as "red flags" which parents or professionals can use to identify that there might be a problem and then spend time with the child getting more information. Some of the behaviors exhibited by children such as "sexual behavior with peers, toys, or animals; sexual language or knowledge that is new or atypical for a given child; or physical trauma to the genitals are all most likely to be caused by sexual abuse." (p. 25-26). He stresses that observation of these signs should be followed up in *all* cases by the parent or caretaker to investigate the cause. Once child sexual abuse is suspected, it must be reported to the appropriate agencies.

Conte (1986) also stresses that "sometimes none of these alert symptoms will be present and yet the child will have been abused" (p. 24). In a study by Conte, Berliner, and Schuerman (1986) it was found that while "the average number of signals or symptoms in evidence was 3.5", 21 percent of the known victims did not exhibit any of these symptoms (cited in Conte, 1986). Mian et al. (1986) reported that 30 percent of the children under six seen at Toronto's Sick Kids Hospital who had disclosed sexual abuse exhibited strictly behavioral symptoms, 12 percent had a combination of physical and behavioral symptoms, and 26 percent of the children had no symptoms. Again, this runs counter to the belief that physical symptoms should be present for a complaint to be substantiated.

It has been suggested that there are problems with applying these lists of indicators to children with developmental disabilities. Davies (06/87) has asserted that many of the symptoms of child sexual abuse are the behaviors of non-victimized children with developmental disabilities. Cole (1986) has also suggested that "the emotional reactions and adjustments of someone who has been denied his or her personal integrity by being assaulted are the same as those of someone who has been denied personal integrity by being institutionalized. Because of the denial of freedom, personal decision-making, privacy, economics, independence, and decreased feelings of personal strength, many persons who have been institutionalized share outward characteristics which indicate a history of abuse. This makes recognition somewhat difficult at times." (p. 82) Until research confirms these symptoms for all children regardless of disability, it would be unwise to assume that they do not apply. Berliner's qualifications mentioned earlier, especially watching for changes in behavior, will likely be found to be the best indicator of abuse. Clinical data presented in several articles has documented cases in which changes of behavior matching those on Sgroi's list, did occur in the victims with developmental disabilities following the assault (Bernstein, 1985; PACER, 1986; Longo & Gochenour, 1981).

Behavioral symptoms and to a lesser extent the physical symptoms of sexual abuse will be missed if parents and caregivers do not know what to look for. In addition, if these caregivers hold negative and/or stereotypical beliefs about children with disabilities, they may attribute behaviors to the disability when they are really the result of sexual abuse. An example of this would be the constant reference in the literature on the sexuality of people with a mental handicap to problems of public masturbation and disrobing (Simonds, 1980; Coleman & Murphy, 1980; Foxx, 1976). While it is clear that many of these instances are the result of inadequate sex education, lack of privacy, and restrictions of sexual expression in institutions, the possibility that some of these children might have been sexually abused is *never* considered. In a daycare or school environment in which the children were not labelled, it would be unlikely that identical behaviors would be punished or dismissed. Vigilanti (undated) is the only author known to date who has summarized the symptoms exhibited by the victims with intellectual impairments in her own practice. They were, "regression to more infantile behaviors, bed-wetting, eating disorders, acting-out attention getting or delinquent behaviors, recurrent physical complaints, self-mutilation, excessive masturbation, depression, withdrawal into fantasy life or some type of dissociative state, frequent genital infections, hyperactive or agitated behaviors, suicidal preoccupations or gestures and hysterical seizure activity" (p. 9). Obviously, symptoms/effects of this magnitude must be addressed and dealt with appropriately if the child/adolescent is to recover and achieve a healthy outlook on life and sexuality.

Results of discovery/disclosure of sexual abuse

It has been shown that identification of "masked" symptoms can lead to discovery of sexual abuse and disclosures by children. In these cases, the doctor/nurse/social worker has followed up the physical/behavioral symptoms due to suspicion of abuse which makes the subsequent disclosure credible. In other situations in which the child discloses without support or prompting, the report may not be believed or responded to. Hard (1986), in an ingenious addition to her study, asked the individuals with developmental disabilities who said they had told someone following the abuse, what happened following their disclosure. Figure 4 shows the results of this line of questioning. Remarkable sex differences were revealed. Over half of the females who disclosed were not believed while all of the males who disclosed were believed. The ability of the disclosure to prevent the continuation of the abuse was also linked to the individual's gender (see Figure 5). Disclosures stopped the abuse from reoccurring in 100 percent of the cases for males, and in 75 percent of the cases for females who were believed. In situations where women disclosed but were not believed, the abuse continued in 55 percent of the cases. This study suggests that sexism is an important factor involved in whether a child or adolescent's disclosure is believed. It also stresses the importance of protection following disclosure particularly for girls.

False reports. The data discussed previously points to the issue of adult's beliefs that children and adolescents do not tell the truth about sexual abuse. It must be remembered that when children disclose, they are not "reporting" or "making allegations", rather they are saying what happened to them (Gossage, 17/12/86). And as discussed earlier few children disclose their abuse under any circumstances. Jones (1985; cited in Conte, 1986) investigated 576 allegations of child sexual abuse and found that less than 8 percent of the complaints were false. Of these false reports, only one quarter were made by children, the rest were made by a parent or other adult. Conte (1986) stresses that few instances are completely fabricated and suggests that we should view the statements as we do the reports of other witnesses, as differentially reliable, biased, accurate. "There is no evidence that many children willfully make false allegations or misinterpret appropriate adult-child contact as sexual abuse and subsequently make a false report." (Conte, 1986, p. 13). Lefkowitz (06/87) points out that there is no correlation between age and honesty, just as there are some adults who lie, some children also lie. However it is unlikely that a child can fabricate something which is outside their daily realm. She suggests that some cases of "false reports" were the result of a child's inappropriate exposure to pornography rather than acted out sexual abuse. Thus the child's "inappropriate sexual knowledge" was accurately assessed. False reports or allegations within the legal system are estimated to be as frequent or infrequent as false reports of other crimes. When they do occur the report has normally been made by an adult, not a child. In most cases children will minimize the abuse rather than exaggerate it, therefore errors made in disclosure involve errors of omission rather than commission (Lefkowitz, 06/87; Croezen, 06/87).

There is no evidence that children with developmental disabilities are any less reliable in the disclosures they make than anyone else although research on this is lacking. Blomberg (06/87) has suggested that as functioning decreases the ability to lie also decreases. She also stated that in her opinion, lying is less common in children and adolescents with developmental disabilities who do not have behavior problems. Stigall (06/87) went further suggesting that children with intellectual impairments would make good witnesses because in her experience they do not lie. The issue around false reports that stands out for Hyman (17/07/87) is the identification of the perpetrator. She suggests that due to fear of the real perpetrator, the child with an intellectual impairment who is questioned about the abuse, may purposefully identify the wrong perpetrator. In these cases there is no denial that the abuse occurred, or incorrect information about the abuse given, the child simply says that the offender was a different person. This is most common, says Hyman (17/07/87), in instances of abuse by a family member, particularly a father. Hyman has found that by questioning the child about all other aspects of the abuse except "who is the perpetrator" she is able to get a pretty good idea of who the person is. Then when she finally asks the child the question, the child less often identifies the wrong person, and Hyman knows whether it is a correct answer. This kind of an error could be crucial in two ways. First, the wrong person might be arrested for the abuse. Secondly, if the evidence does not support the child's story, it will be assumed that she lied about the *abuse* not simply the identification of the perpetrator.

Sgroi (1982) presents the most detailed and well accepted methods of "validation" of sexual abuse cases and while she does not include children with intellectual impairments explicitly, it would be easily adaptable to their situation with few modifications. (See Sgroi, 1982 for more details). This type of validation procedure is crucial in assessing the counselling needs of the victim as well as being a necessary part of preparation for the court process. Sgroi (1982) stresses "Determining the validity of an allegation of child sexual abuse is first and foremost a matter of belief. You either believe the child's story or you do not. If you require that there be corroboration of the child's story by physical evidence, witnesses, or a confession by the perpetrators, you will turn many cases into 'noncases' " (p. 69).

4

EFFECTS OF SEXUAL ABUSE

Theories explaining psychological effects

The effects of sexual abuse on children are as varied in their manifestations as the children. Theories of effects attempt to explain and predict these differences between children and situations. While these theories have never been applied specifically to children with developmental disabilities, there is no evidence to suggest that the experience of these children would be outside the range of effects being discussed. It will therefore be assumed that effects will vary from child to child, and situation to situation; sometimes independent of the child's disability, sometimes partially dependent on it.

Some authors suggest that the effects of abuse depend on a variety of demographic and situational dynamics such as, the age of the victim, the presence or absence of physical force, and the duration of the abuse (Russell, 1984; Finkelhor, 1979). Finkelhor and Browne (1985) have broken from that line of thinking postulating instead "four traumagenic dynamics" which attempt to explain the etiology of the effects of child sexual abuse. While this theory has not yet been empirically tested, it is a useful framework within which the effects of sexual abuse can be discussed. Each of the four dynamics will be discussed as they relate to children with developmental disabilities.

1) traumatic sexualization   is "a process in which a child's sexuality (including both sexual feelings and sexual attitudes) is shaped in a developmentally inappropriate and interpersonally inappropriate and interpersonally dysfunctional fashion as a result of sexual abuse" (Finkelhor & Browne, 1985, p. 531).[8] Summit points out that due to the extreme secrecy surrounding sexual abuse of children, children are "entirely dependent on the intruder for whatever reality is assigned to the experience" (p. 181). For children who lack sex education or are isolated from other information, (this has been shown previously to be the case for many children with developmental disabilities) this dynamic is likely to be exaggerated.

2) betrayal   is "the dynamic by which children discover that someone on whom they were vitally dependent has caused them harm" (Finkelhor & Browne, 1985, p. 531). As the child with an intellectual impairment is more likely to be abused by someone who is their caretaker (See Prevalence of sexual abuse) this dynamic will almost always be present.

3) powerlessness   this is "the process in which the child's will, desires, and sense of efficacy are continually contravened" (Finkelhor & Browne, 1985, p. 532). This dynamic may be exaggerated in children whose will, desires and sense of efficacy are already being undermined or ignored, such as in the case of some institutionalized children (Wooden, 1976).

4) stigmatization   "refers to the negative connotations . . . that are communicated to the child around the experiences and that then become incorporated into the child's self-image" (p. 532). Summit (1983) elaborates saying, "a child with no knowledge or awareness of sex and even with no pain or embarrassment from the sexual experience itself will still be stigmatized by a sense of badness and danger from the pervasive secrecy" (p. 181). This is a strong statement refuting the idea that children with intellectual impairments will not be affected by abuse if they do not know what is happening to them. This dynamic would still be present.

Short term effects in childhood

Numerous articles have been written documenting the effects of sexual abuse on children (Friedrich & Reams, in press; Katan, 1973;

Bender & Blau, 1937; Elonen & Zwarensteyn, 1975; Blumberg, 1979; Summit, 1983). The effects which are commonly noted will be briefly discussed here as they relate to children with developmental disabilities.

Summit (1983) presents a theory of effects labelled the "Child Sexual Abuse Accommodation Syndrome", an understanding of which he suggests "is essential to provide a counter-prejudicial explanation to the otherwise self-camouflaging and self-stigmatizing behavior of the victim" (p. 179). Summit points out that for most children sexual abuse is not a single incident but rather is a repetitive, often increasingly demanding pattern of sexual demands. As a result of constant victimization and the accompanying helplessness, Summit suggests that the child attempts to achieve a sense of control by developing internal ways to cope. For example, a child may rationalize that she deserved the abuse because she is bad, or that she is protecting her younger brothers and sisters by being the father's victim. Outward expressions of rage such as self-mutilation (Summit, 1983), suicide attempts (Goodwin, 1981; Summit, 1983), and promiscuity (Summit, 1983; Silbert & Pines, 1981), might also occur. Summit (1983) suggests that the male victim may react differently as he may be less tolerant of the helplessness and seek to victimize others as a way of controlling the situation. Summit stresses that all of these effects are "part of the survival skills of the child" (p. 186).

In a review of the wide clinical and empirical literature, Browne and Finkelhor (1986) report that the most common effects which children experience are: fear, anger and hostility, guilt and shame, depression, anxiety and distress. Inappropriate sexual activities such as "open masturbation, excessive sexual curiosity, and frequent exposure of the genitals" were also noted.

The only published report of effects experienced by children with developmental disabilities is by Varley (1984). He had three "mentally retarded" female patients who were diagnosed with schizophreniform psychoses.[9] Once the psychoses had been treated, sexual assault and abuse was disclosed by all three women. Varley suggests that girls with intellectual impairments are inadequately prepared for their emerging sexuality and less able to defend themselves against sexual attacks. He suggests that if anything the likelihood of severe psychological trauma might be more likely.

Long term effects into Adulthood

Another way of investigating the effects of sexual abuse is to examine those effects which persist into adulthood. Normally these are investigated by comparing adults who have been victimized with those who have not on a variety of mental health measures. When this is done, it is found that adults who were abused as children are more depressed (Bagley & Ramsay, 1986; Peters, 1984), more self-destructive (Briere, 1984, cited in Finkelhor & Assoc., 1986; Bagley & Ramsay, 1986; Herman, 1981), more anxious (Briere, 1984, cited in Browne & Finkelhor, 1986; Bagley & Ramsay, 1986), and have more negative self-concept (Bagley & Ramsay, 1985) than non-victimized adults. Other effects which have been documented (and are summarized in Browne and Finkelhor (1986)) deal with difficulties in relating to their own children and to partners of the opposite sex. In addition, a disturbing finding which has been found repeatedly is the phenomenon of "revictimization" whereby women who were abused as children are more likely to be victimized later in life by someone else (Russell, 1984; Briere, 1984, cited in Browne & Finkelhor, 1986). Revictimization has also been found by Hard (1986) in her sample of women with developmental disabilities who were sexually abused. Her data suggest that revictimization is not as common for male victims. Hyman (17/07/87) stated that it was extremely rare for her to find a woman with intellectual impairments who had been victimized only once. (See Russell (1986) for a complete discussion of revictimization).

To summarize, the psychological effects of child sexual abuse in the short term can be seen to be 'pathological' in between 20 and 40 percent of the abused children seen by clinicians (Browne & Finkelhor, 1986, p. 72). The long terms effects, those which persist into adulthood, seem to severely impair less than 20 percent of the adults who were abused as children (Browne & Finkelhor, 1986). More subtle negative effects, both short and long term, are commonly documented, however, they are less likely to come to the attention of a clinician. The view that sexual abuse in childhood is not damaging, while still held by some (e.g., Johnson & Kempton, 1981), can no longer be supported by the empirical literature.

5

TREATMENT FOR THE CHILD SEXUAL ABUSE SURVIVOR

Medical Treatment

Medical examinations are a crucial step once a child has been identified as a victim of sexual abuse. The most obvious reason is to check the child for injuries or infections which need to be treated. This type of examination can, in some cases, also provide physical evidence of the abuse for later legal proceedings. While the number of children with physical injuries is small, new techniques for detecting torn tissue (McCauley, Gorman, & Guzinski, 1986) and more aggressive testing for venereal disease (Silber & Controni, 1983) even in the absence of symptoms make it more likely that physical evidence will be found. Another important reason for the medical examination is to reassure the child that she is not permanently "damaged" by the assault (Conte, 1986).

Psychological Treatment

Psychological treatment for the victim of child sexual abuse is a complicated process which varies depending on whether the abuse is intrafamilial or extrafamilial as well as the perspective of the therapist/clinician/social worker. In the case of intrafamilial abuse, the entire family is usually treated. Forseth and Brown (1981) surveyed treatment programs in the U.S. and found a wide variety of program types being employed. Their conclusion was that an interdisciplinary approach was the most effective type, usually including family therapy, individual therapy, and offender groups.[10] Treatment of extrafamilial abuse, on the other hand, is normally restricted to treatment of the victim of the abuse.

Much information on the treatment of sexual abuse is now commonly available. Reference books such as Sgroi (1982) and Burgess, Groth, Holmstrom, and Sgroi (1978) are the best sources of information for treatment of extrafamilial sexual abuse. Specialized books such as Mayer (1983) are excellent resources for information on the treatment of intrafamilial sexual abuse. Very little information is available which refers specifically to the child victim with an intellectual impairment. Baladerian, Dankowski & Jackson (1986) have put together the only known package of materials for the victims of sexual abuse with developmental disabilities (with two reading levels), her parents and professionals. It is called *Survivor* and is an excellent self-help resource. Szymanski and Jansen (1980) stress that treatment of individuals with developmental disabilities need not be substantially different from that for non-disabled individuals. A reference by Johnson and Kempton (1981) which from its title appeared promising, is not at all helpful as it denies virtually all harm to a child victim and encourages the belief that children seek out molestation. For example, it suggests that "The girls sometimes initiate or at least encourage the behavior with esteemed adult males. There is no evidence of emotional trauma brought about by these experiences." (p. 157). A chapter by Burgess and Holmstrom (1978) is the only known reference which deals well with the special needs of counselling handicapped victims. The guidelines were developed with reference to adolescent rape victims and therefore would require some adaptation for children. These guidelines (techniques) are so good that they deserve reproduction here (see Figure 6). Longo and Gochenour (1981) also present some insights for working with disabled assault victims although these are limited in both depth and number.

6

ACCESSIBILITY OF SERVICES

No information has been compiled to suggest what services are accessible to victims of child sexual abuse with intellectual impairments. In fact discussing accessibility of services for individuals with the most severe disabilities is not necessary. They have no access themselves especially when they are institutionalized and do not have advocates. This author recognizes that some victims have no autonomy currently and are completely dependent on the knowledge, expertise, and wishes of their caretakers. As such, the discussion of accessibility will include those victims who could access standard services if they were aware of their existence.

It is useful to adapt the standards of accessibility of victim services developed by Per-Lee (1981) with relation to physical disabilities to the needs of victims with intellectual impairments. First, is there 'real access'? Is the service accessible to those with developmental disabilities in an absolute way, that is, if an individual with a handicap arrived at the service would they be helped or not? Included in a list of services which are not accessible would be those agencies which, due to the existing overburdening of their services, are not willing to take on any clients with "special needs" or from a "special group"; those which refer all individuals with developmental disabilities to other agencies which "specialize in those problems" (meaning the disability not the abuse); those whose individual counsellors "wouldn't know what to do or how to handle it" and so suggest a referral, etc. The second test of accessibility is "perceived accessibility". If a service-providing agency is willing to see children or adolescents with developmental disabilities but does no outreach to the specific community then it is likely that they will be perceived as inaccessible and will see very few disabled people. As Per-Lee (1981) points out, many individuals with handicaps are used to being shut out of society and will not assume a service is accessible until explicitly informed that it is.

It is difficult to assess accessibility and to establish how many people with disabilities are currently being (or have previously been) helped. One reason is that agencies do not routinely test clients for their level of functioning[11] and so they rely on their own estimates of the person's abilities. Unless the person brought in by an advocate, mentions their group home or special school, or states that they have a developmental disabilities, the person who is doing the intake may not be able to recognize the disability. In addition, most intake forms do not request the counsellor to state whether the person has a physical or mental handicap, so even when the presence of a disability is known, the agency will not be able to access that information. Thus, statistics are very hard to gather. It is also difficult to expect agencies to volunteer information which would make their discrimination obvious, unless there was some incentive to do so.

Medical Accessibility

Hospitals are probably the most uniformly accessible facilities. Hospital personnel are used to seeing a wide variety of patients as well as addressing a variety of issues. Toronto's Hospital for Sick Children for example, has seen sexually abused children with developmental disabilities. However they do not keep statistics on children's disabilities so actual numbers are not available. This hospital has its own treatment program and does treat cases involving victims of intrafamilial abuse with developmental disabilities at the hospital. This would involve intervention with the entire family in most cases. In the case of extrafamilial abuse, the victims with an intellectual impairment would usually be referred to a specialized agency, such as Surrey Place, West End Creche, or Sacred Heart, with consultation maintained. The Sexual Assault Unit at Women's College Hospital in Toronto has an age restriction so they see only women over 16 years of age. Nannarone (05/87) stated that the unit had seen women with developmental disabilities in their emergency services but had not as yet been used in their follow up counselling and support service. They have not done any outreach to the handicapped community. They would be willing to act as consultants to any agencies for the intellectually impaired wishing to address sexual assault.

It would be naive and perhaps unethical to suggest medical intervention with children and adolescents with intellectual impairments without addressing briefly their past experience with the medical profession. Abuses by doctors in the form of overmedication (Duffet, 06/87; Sank & Lafleche, 1984), impatience and callousness (Sank & Lafleche, 1984), have been stressed by some people working in the field. It has also been noted that many adolescent girls with developmental disabilities are not afforded regular gynecological exams which are the norm for other adolescent girls (Sank & Lafleche, 1984), while others have been sterilized without their consent (Rioux, 1979). It would be extremely harmful to the child or adolescent to be examined following abuse (and at all other times) by someone who is not careful, patient, and considerate and who does not explain what they are doing. Education of medical personnel about the health needs of the person with an intellectual impairment would go a long way to solving this problem.

Child Protection

Schilling, Kirkham and Schinke (1986) have recently reviewed the literature on the provision of services to children with developmental disabilities by child protection workers. They found that children with mental handicaps were underrepresented in the case loads of workers even though they appear to be at higher risk for all types of abuse. The majority of caseworkers surveyed could not recall even one child with developmental disabilities on their caseload. The workers believed that they were already skilled at detecting intellectual impairment and showed little interest in continued education to increase their knowledge and skills in dealing with children with intellectual impairments. Camblin (1982) reported that only half of the state child protection agencies he surveyed collected data on handicapping conditions while those who did, often did so in a haphazard and incomplete fashion. Therefore data on the number of children with developmental disabilities receiving protection from sexual abuse are virtually nonexistent. Schilling, Kirkhan and Schinke (1986) suggest that this has occurred due to a "bureaucratic separation" between child welfare organizations and those agencies associated with special disabilities. Therefore, "child protection workers may consider handicapped children outside their responsibility." (p. 22) While CPS workers should not be blamed for a situation which has likely arisen due to bureaucratic factors, training of the workers may be one of the most vulnerable places for change to begin.

Krents (06/87) has reported that less than half of the child protection workers in New York State are familiar with the needs of disabled children either through their education or their personal experience. Data on the Canadian situation are not available, however, the situation appears to be similar. Canadian child protection workers are not provided with special training which would make their situation remarkably different. This would not be a problem if it meant only that workers had to learn quickly. Instead it often means the quick referral of a child to a "specialized agency" perhaps not capable or experienced in handling sexual abuse cases. The possibility for children to fall between the cracks is great (Krents, 05/87). Some governments have recognized these problems and are attempting to remedy them. Krents at the Lexington Centre is currently training all new protection workers to work with children with various disabilities.

Rape Crisis Centres

Rape crisis centres normally see adult or adolescent victims of rape and survivors of sexual abuse. While they do not see many children who have been sexually abused, their approach to counselling may put them in a unique position to handle clients with intellectual impairments. The feminist model on which most rape crisis centres' counselling services are based is one which gives control back to the victim (Shaman, 05/87). Individual differences between women are expected and accommodated therefore a disability is not viewed as a limitation (Duffet, 05/87). Counselling adapts to the woman's situation. Shaman (05/87) of Seattle Rape Relief, believes that counsellors need to understand the issues surrounding disabilities, the communication problems which may be present in some cases, and the services available in the community. While some counsellors may not be sure of their ability to "handle" the client with a developmental disability, it has been suggested that a number of workshops done by people working in the field of mental handicap could bring the centre to a place where clients with intellectual impairments were welcomed (Fifield, 1986). The Toronto Rape Crisis Centre has had several inhouse training workshops of this sort (Martin, 05/87; Finkler, 04/87). Other counselling centres which have an eclectic approach to counselling could also be quite easily converted to greater accessibility by educational workshops.

The problems in service accessibility which have the greatest impact are two-fold. The first is the complete inaccessibility of services for certain populations of people. The second problem appears to derive from the attitudes and beliefs of people working in the area of sexual abuse. Individuals may be open to counselling the survivor of abuse with an intellectual impairment but may not believe that the victim can be included in the "normal" treatment program established by the service. While this may be true in some cases, this belief may be due simply to a lack of familiarity with people with mental handicaps. Duffet (06/87) did not view the victims with developmental disabilities she saw at the rape crisis centre as needing special services. They received individual counselling and were included in a self-help group which mixed disabled and non-disabled women. Duffet reported that the group was very successful and will probably be started again next year. This is the only known case of a fully accessible counselling program in Ontario which has both real and perceived accessibility. This kind of counselling approach may not be suitable for all women, however its existence along with other options might afford the victim of abuse a choice of services. While this group was run with adult victims of assault and abuse there is no reason that with some planning, integrated groups of child victims could not be run by other treatment centres. For children who do not perform well in groups, individual therapy can also be adapted for their needs.

7

PREVENTION OF SEXUAL ABUSE

Prevention programs for sexual abuse are often assumed to be aimed at the children who are at risk for abuse, however, that is just one aspect of prevention. Finkelhor and Araji (1983) have identified three target audiences for abuse prevention: 1) children, 2) parents and, 3) professionals. In the case of children with developmental disabilities a fourth target audience can be added, the institution,[12] which is in the unique position of having numerous professionals and staff all interacting with children. Each target audience will be addressed with the child victim with an intellectual impairment in mind. Anderson (06/87) stresses that there is "no quick fix" available for the prevention of child sexual abuse.

Children

Sex education. Sex education for children and adolescents with developmental disabilities is advocated for many reasons, only one of which is for the prevention of abuse (Baladerian, 1976; Forchuk et al., 1984; Green, 1983; Geist, Knudsen & Sorenson, 1979; Sengstock & Vergason, 1970). It is believed to be a necessary part of any prevention effort (Davies, 06/87; Anderson, 05/87; Blomberg, 06/87), especially since information on sexuality appears to be particularly limited in populations with developmental disabilities (Edmonson & Wish, 1975; Hall, Morris, & Barker, 1973; Hall & Morris, 1976; Edmonson, McCombs, & Wish, 1979).

There is some consensus amongst sex educators about the nature of the programs which should be offered to children and adolescents with intellectual impairments. First, the child needs to be aware of his/her body and its functionings. A child who has been given education about her/his body will be better able to describe any instances of sexual abuse which do occur in terminology which can be understood (Baladerian, 1985). But "plumbing" information alone is not sufficient. Sex education should also include information about sexuality including sexual ethics, rights, and responsibilities, varied according to the age of the child (Baladerian, 1985). A discussion of rights and responsibilities can set the stage for later discussion of abuse and assault.

Another point that has been stressed by people working in the field is that all sex education programs should be adapted to take into account both the chronological age and the functioning level of the children/adolescents for whom it is intended (Blomberg, 1986;). The program should not just be a watered down version of regular sex education but rather one which has been adapted through means which have been proven to be good teaching tools for children with developmental disabilities such as the use of pictures and concrete examples. Education programs should ideally be integrated into the curriculum or spread over a period of time and evaluated both at the end and some time later for retention.

Hard (1986) has demonstrated convincingly the impact of sex education on the ability of children to avoid victimization. She defined sex education as being any education on sexuality over five hours in duration (06/87). Seventy-two percent of the individuals interviewed "had received no sex education through parents, care providers or the school system." (p. 6) Figure 7 represents the amount of sexual abuse broken down by sex and sex education. These charts clearly illustrate the impact of sex education on sexual abuse particularly for females. All of the women without sex education had been abused, while only 12 percent of those with sex education had been abused. Sex education was also related to lower levels of abuse in males, although the relationship was not as dramatic.

Difficulties in establishing sex education programs for children have been well documented in the past. But as Shore (1982) asserted, "there is no such thing as no sex education" (p. 176). Even in institutions where the flow of information is extremely restricted, children gain access to pornography (Sengstock & Vergason, 1970), may witness the sexual abuse of other children (Duffet, 05/87), and may experience abuse themselves (Wooden, 1976; Musick, 1981). Duffet (05/87) and Hard (1986) have both presented anecdotal data in which women with developmental disabilities learned everything they knew about sex from their abusive experiences. This situation is intolerable.

Self-protection. Self-protection training for children can involve both physical and non-physical self-defense. Physical self-defense programs for individuals with intellectual impairments have been offered in the past primarily to adolescents and adults (MacPherson, 1984). WENDO, a women's self-defense program offers programs for all girls and women over the age of 12. These programs have also been found to be empowering for previous victims of assault.

The more common approach for children has been special sexual abuse prevention programs which incorporate assertiveness training with learning about types of touch, coercion, and abuse. Within the past few years, several programs have been adapted specifically for children with developmental disabilities. A list of these programs along with their appropriateness for different groups of children is included in Appendix A. Most of the programs are aimed at children with mild to moderate disabilities. Only one (NO-GO-TELL) would be appropriate for children under six years of age. Since only limited evaluations have been carried out thus far (e.g., Fisher & Field, 1985; Cowardin, 1986) it is impossible to recommend one program over another.

Many individuals working in prevention stress the need both for prior sex education and positive sexuality training before prevention programs so that children do not associate all touch with fear and exploitation (Davies, 05/87; Fifield, 1986).

Anderson (19/05/87) and others have stressed that much to many parents' and professionals' surprise, children and adolescents with developmental disabilities have no difficulty grasping complex concepts such as manipulation and tricking, as long as the material is presented in concrete manner. Role plays seem to work particularly well with children with developmental disabilities (Davies, 05/87; Anderson, 19/05/87). In this way children can be taught the "avoidance, resistance, and help seeking techniques" (Finkelhor & Araji, 1983, p. 14) that they need to protect themselves against sexual abuse.

Environmental changes. In prevention programs, children and adolescents are taught help-seeking behavior as well as assertiveness. It has been pointed out by people working with victims with intellectual impairments that in some cases this information would have been useless, since the child did not have access to private use of a phone, or private time alone with a worker other than the one who was abusing them (Duffet, 05/87). Environmental changes to provide children with privacy and a route for disclosure are a necessary part of any effective prevention program.

Parents

Parents of children with developmental disabilities may be in a unique position to be offered education programs as they appear as a group to be more interested in sex education topics than the parents of other children (Goodman, Budner, & Lesh, 1971, cited in Johnson & Kempton, 1981, p. 72). No prevention program known to date has attempted to educate fathers against sexually abusing their daughters. Prevention programs for parents usually involve some of the following features: (a) sex education to correct sexual misinformation particularly as it relates to their children, (b) explanation of the sexual abuse prevention programs offered to their children to help them reinforce what their children are learning, and (c) information on signs and symptoms to increase the likelihood of detection of victimization if it does occur. It appears that most of the prevention material aimed at parents has been given in written form, in articles in parents' magazines (e.g., Murphy & Della Corte, 1987), or in pamphlets distributed to certain groups of parents (e.g, foster parents, Gil (1982)). Finkelhor and Araji (1983) noted that while many films were available to teach prevention to children, one has not been developed to teach parents how to teach their children prevention skills. The need for this type of prevention is demonstrated by a study by Finkelhor (1984) which found that 61 percent of parents believed that their neighborhoods were safer than average. While parents of children with intellectual impairments may be more prone to seeing their child as at risk for sexual abuse than other parents, parents who do not recognize the risk to their children, will not be as able to adequately protect them or to deal with the effects.

Professionals

According to Finkelhor and Araji (1983) professionals working with children must be educated to accomplish six goals. First, they must be able to understand the basic concepts involved in the sexual abuse of children and must be able to communicate these adequately to children. Second, they must be trained to be sensitive to the signs and symptoms of sexual abuse so that they can intervene quickly. Third, they must be able to probe a child gently to obtain information about the child's possible sexual abuse. Fourth, they should be trained how to respond to disclosure of sexual abuse so that they do not harm or shut down the child who has disclosed. Fifth, they must be up to date and knowledgeable of the referrals which are appropriate in sexual abuse cases. And sixth, they must "be able to communicate . . . the basic concepts of prevention" (p. 9) to others. Obviously, the need for people who work with children with developmental disabilities to accomplish all six of these goals differs according to their function, however, most of the skills could be taught in a fairly short time. Some attempts by professionals to address their role in prevention are now being made. For example, see Jenny, Sutherland, and Sandahl (1986) for a plan proposed by pediatric health workers.

Finkelhor and Araji (1983) point out the possibility that children may in actuality have very little control over whether or not they are abused therefore the education of professionals may be the most important point at which to aim prevention programs. The benefits of such a focus as suggested by Finkelhor and Araji (1983) would be: earlier identification of sexual abuse, fast and beneficial responses to disclosures, immediate assistance and referrals, and duplicated prevention messages to children and parents by other professionals.

Institutions

Sex education and prevention programming. The provision of sex education in residential facilities is now virtually universally accepted as necessary for the physical and mental health of the residents (Geist, Knudsen, & Sorenson, 1979; Friedman, 1972; Sengstock & Vergason, 1970; Edmonson & Wish, 1975; Hall, Morris & Barker, 1973; Hall & Morris, 1976; Edmonson, McCombs & Wish, 1979; Coleman & Murphy, 1980). Many of these authors pointed out that the residents were being prepared for deinstitutionalization and

should be prepared with respect to sexuality as well. While acceptance for the concept of sex education has increased dramatically
over past years, in practice this acceptance may be very limited and
of a superficial nature. Coleman and Murphy (1980) point out that
while "the majority of facilities approved of and provided sex education, very few allowed the expression of sexuality except through
masturbation. This mixed message is likely to be quite confusing to
the mentally retarded person and could possibly lead to confusion in
the whole area of sexuality" (p. 274-275). Coleman and Murphy
(1980) also state that "adverse reactions" were listed by the institutions they surveyed "as both an initial problem and a negative side
effect" of the implementation of sex education programs. These
contradictions between the sex education programs and the general
environment must be alleviated if children are to receive the message that sexuality can be a healthy, positive experience.

Shore (1982) has listed the variables which enable the successful
insertion of sex education programs into existing programs as being,
"commitment from administration at the highest level, involvement
of staff at the earliest stages and a willingness to move slowly in
light of the impending resistance that always precedes and accom-
panies change." (p. 180) Careful planning, the use of a tested and
respected program, training sessions for staff, and client, parent and
staff input, would all help to ease the transition from a facility with a
negative sexual environment to one in which healthy attitudes are
encouraged.

Screening of employees.   Screening of employees has often been
utilized as the primary (or only) method of preventing sexual abuse
in residential facilities (Dawson, 06/87). Screening for criminal
records is probably the most common technique. These checks
screen out convicted child molesters and sex offenders. Unfortunately, as mentioned previously, few cases of child sexual assault
are ever reported, fewer make it to the police, fewer still reach the
court system, and only a miniscule number result in convictions
which would show up on a person's record. Therefore only a few
perpetrators would be screened out by a criminal record check. In
Ontario, in the past employers could check the Central Abuse Registry to screen employees, however this is no longer possible (Dawson, 06/87). As Rose (1986) has pointed out, even with a screening
process in place, offenders have been hired. Reliance on this method
for prevention may be harmful as it gives the illusion of protecting
children from offenders but does not actually do so. Criminal

records checks should be done with the knowledge that they will rarely detect perpetrators.

Other methods of screening, such as the use of questionnaires which tap proclivity to abuse and other psychological measures, have been suggested by one author (Gil, 1979). Screening for proclivity to abuse has not yet been validated but would be an alternative to existing techniques. However, it must be stressed that no screening process should substitute for a prevention program.

Policies and Procedures. Three types of sexual abuse have been documented in institutions, each of which requires a different approach. First, there is perhaps the most common type of abuse, which is sexual neglect created by the institutional setting in which residents are routinely deprived of their sexual rights. Solutions include deinstitutionalization, sex education programs, increased privacy, and the addressing of sexual issues within the institution. This type of sexual abuse is beyond the scope of this document but has been addressed articulately elsewhere (see for example, Shore, 1980; Szymanski and Jansen, 1983; Hirayama, 1979).

The second type of sexual abuse documented in the literature is the abuse of residents by other residents. Case reports of these types of attacks are common. The victims appear to be both male and female while the perpetrators are most commonly male residents (Shaman, 05/87; Duffet, 05/87). The offenders are also usually either higher functioning (Szymanski & Jansen, 1983), or dual diagnosed aggressive males (Bernstein, 1985; Hirayama, 1979; Blomberg, 05/87; PACER, 1986). While institutions are moving away from policies which overcontrol the sexual behavior of residents, they are now likely to avoid explicit policies or guidelines altogether (Hirayama, 1979; Shore, 1980; Szymanski & Jansen, 1983). This means that rules and their enforcement are left to the whim of staff members and are not clearly laid out for the residents. Shore (1980) has suggested the establishment of "adhoc, interdisciplinary, sexual issues committees" which would develop "policies and procedures for harmful sexual activities" as well as "policies and procedures for addressing training and program planning for appropriate sexual expression of residents" (p. 181) as one solution. Sex education and prevention programs which include a sexual rights and responsibilities component have been shown to help some residents to understand the inappropriateness and harmfulness of their actions (Forchuk et al., 1984; WAR, undated). Several instances have been documented in which sex offenders with developmental disabilities were returned to facilities for the intellectually impaired as there were no prison or juvenile facilities suitable for them. They received no treatment and continued to offend against other residents (Murphy, Coleman & Haynes, 1983; Bernstein, 1985). This is an example of the dismal failure of the system to provide help both to the victim and the perpetrator. Whether or not criminal proceedings are followed, perpetrators (residents) must receive treatment, and their victims or potential victims must receive protection and/or treatment. To do less is to contribute to the abuse.

The third type of abuse documented in the literature are the cases of staff members or assigned caretakers who abuse residents either through the use of coercion or the illusion of a consensual relationship (Longo & Gocheneur, 1981). Again, few residential facilities have explicit policies or guidelines for sexual contact between staff and residents (Shore, 1980; Hiriyama, 1979; Szymanski & Jansen, 1983; Dawson, 06/87). Dawson (06/87) has suggested that explicit rules be made to enable staff to judge what is acceptable behavior. His suggestions for topics to be covered in these rules are presented in Figure 8. However, some educators have stressed that staff members may overreact to such policies with a "no-touch" response. Anderson (06/87) stresses the importance of fighting against the paranoia of the "no touch" contingent so that children are not harmed by the removal of all contact. Shore (1980) agrees saying "the set of guidelines for sexual contact between staff and residents should be equally as proscriptive, discriminating between physical and sexual contact along with examples of each and outlining the consequences of actions that do not conform to the policies and procedures." (p. 182) In this way, the concerns of staff members that they will be persecuted for necessary and affectionate touching will be addressed.

Dawson (06/87) recently presented an outline of procedures which could help institutions to avoid complaints against them. These procedures would serve the additional function of providing children and adolescents with better service. In this respect, Dawson's procedures (presented in Figure 9) are useful.

The suggestions for case preparation have been put forward by Dawson due to the finding that many children in care have special needs which put them at higher risk for abuse (Gil, 1982b; 1979; Dawson, undated; PACER, 1986). It has been suggested that training staff to deal with the types of behavior children may exhibit may prevent further abuse. For example, it has been shown previously that girls who have been sexually abused may exhibit symptoms of precocious sexual behavior toward adult males. If male workers were prepared for this reality they may be able to handle the situation in such a way as to avoid further victimizing a traumatized child. While male staff members should already know that sexual activity with children/adolescents in their care is inappropriate, some obviously do not unless told so explicitly.

Procedures and guidelines make behavior codes explicit to staff and ensure that they know what behavior is considered acceptable within the facility. Asking staff to have witnesses and to keep notes about certain interactions may be a good idea, however, it may also increase paranoia about false complaints. As mentioned earlier, false complaints are extremely unusual. Dawson's third procedural suggestion is probably the best, which is to encourage parents, workers, and the facility to be open and honest about things that happen. One policy which would assist in the implementation of this suggestion would be the opening of institutions to parents and other support groups. A further benefit would derive from the fact that children who maintain some contact with their parents have been shown to be at lower risk for abuse (Dawson, undated). Exit interviews with children leaving the facility are also an excellent idea suggested by Dawson (06/87) for finding out how the facility could be improved and identifying problem staff members.

Another problem encountered by institutions and addressed in Dawson's procedures, is the fear of bad publicity if sexual abuse comes to light. Responses to allegations of abuse in the past have been varied but one response has been to fire the staff person involved without pressing criminal charges (Dawson, 06/87; Rose, 1986). The inadequacies of this approach are three-fold. First, this informal response does not address the victim's need for a serious response to her disclosure. Shore (1980) has asserted that the failure of staff to respond adequately to a child's disclosure may imply (in the child's mind), that they condone the behavior. More severe trauma may result (Cole, 1980; Summit, 1983). Second, the response does not impress upon the staff member or other staff members the seriousness of sexual abuse of residents and the harm done to them. Thirdly, the offender is given the opportunity (and from anecdotal information, it is evident that he often takes it (Rose, 1984; Dawson, 06/87)) to be hired at another facility[13] where a new group of residents are victimized.

Dawson (06/87) has distinguished between sexually inappropriate behaviours (such as using vulgar language and making inappropriate comments about client's bodies), and sexually abusive behavior (which he defined as illegal sexual behaviors). He believes that the former should be dealt with internally, while the latter should be investigated and dealt with externally. Regardless of the policy held by the individual institution, by law all instances of sexual abuse must be reported. Gil (1979) has suggested that allegations of physical abuse be investigated and dealt with internally whenever possible. In this author's opinion few individuals would be capable of correctly investigating complaints of sexual abuse without specific training. Furthermore, an internal investigation would ensure a delay between the disclosure and reporting to the police and/or child protection which would not be in the best interests of the child. For example, the Ministry of Community and Social Services *Guidelines for the Investigation of Resident Abuse in Facilities for the Mentally Retarded* (1978) order notification of the police at such time as "sufficient evidence exists to substantiate an allegation of physical or sexual abuse" (p. 3). A preliminary investigation done by the staff member in charge would determine whether this condition had been met. This procedure leaves a great deal to the discretion of someone who is a colleague and possible friend of the accused.

Dawson (undated) in a study of abuse in foster homes in Ontario, found that while children were removed from foster homes in most cases and the homes were closed in many, charges were laid in only 10 percent of the cases and reports made to the Central Abuse Registry in only 26 percent of the cases. Obviously, even for social service agencies the desire to handle complaints internally is strong. The likelihood of this occurring in a private facility is probably even greater. This practice must be resisted. The Committee on Disabilities of the ICAN Task Force on Sexual Abuse (1985) surveyed regional centres asking them how they handled and identified abuse cases. Only four out of seven centres responded. In two of the centres staff had been trained specifically in dealing with sexual assault, one centre's staff had received only limited training, while staff at one centre had received none. All of the centres reported alleged child sexual abuse to child protections services, but only two reported them to the police. Durkin (1982) has written of the difficulties in reporting institutional abuse. The reporters often suffer tremendously in their own lives. But as Kline (1976) and Green (1976) have documented, the consequences of failure to report (in various settings) are often disastrous to the child.

Work environment. Several authors have mentioned that the work situation of the care providers in institutional facilities may contribute to child abuse (Dawson, 06/87; Gil, 1979; PACER, 1986). The low pay, shift work, long hours and often nonrewarding work, huge caseloads, and power structures, may all contribute to a situation in which the worker loses their interest in the child's welfare. Dawson (undated) found overloading of foster-care services to be a crucial factor in abuse. It is not clear what role these factors play in sexual abuse however environmental stresses should be taken into account in any prevention effort.

8

SEX OFFENDERS WITH
INTELLECTUAL IMPAIRMENTS

Prevalence of Offenses Committed by
Offenders with Developmental Disabilities

The early literature on sex offenses strongly supported the notion that many sex offenders were of low intelligence.[14] One such article went so far as to suggest: "No one with any criminological experience would attempt to belie the statement that were all of the feeble-minded to be removed from the community the crime picture would change remarkably and, as a matter of fact, a very great number of crimes would no longer be committed or, if they were committed, would be committed so sporadically as not even to constitute social problems." (Selling, 1939, p. 178). He concludes his discussion of sex offenses in particular with the statement that while "all sex offenses cannot be laid at the door of the feebleminded . . . a better intellectual endowment would seem to be a very definite predisposing factor in the prevention of cases of sex offense." (p. 186) While not all writers at the time nor few since have held such an extreme view of the role of individuals who have been labelled mentally retarded in the commission of sex offences, the myth that they are "over-sexed" and potential sex offenders is still fairly common (Hall, 1974).

Activists and professionals who work with individuals with

developmental disabilities have been working to overcome these myths for many years. Especially in the process of deinstitutionalization, community workers have struggled hard to teach the public that males with intellectual impairments are not a risk to their children. The truth is that the majority of men are not sex offenders, but some, with and without intellectual impairments most certainly are. Hyman (17/07/87) has encountered the most resistance in her work with offenders labelled mentally retarded from professionals in the field who do not feel comfortable with people addressing the issue. This is unfortunate. Just as there is nothing inherent in the disability which makes men sex offenders, there is nothing inherent in it which would inoculate them from becoming one.

Some adolescent and adult men with developmental disabilities do sexually abuse their own children (Seagull & Scheurer, 1986; Virkkunen, 1974), while some others sexually abuse other people's children (Whitman & Quinsey, 1981; Stokes, 1964; Murphy, Coleman, & Haynes, 1983). Research on sex offences does not show an unusually high proportion committed by perpetrators with intellectual impairments although there is variability in the findings depending on the methodology used. Gebhard, Gagnon, Pomeroy, and Christenson (1965) reported percentages ranging from 10-20 percent of offenders being labelled "mentally defective" with the highest estimate (20 percent) being found in the heterosexual child molestation situation. Most studies have found that the number of offenders with intellectual impairments is not much above the representation of the disability in the population (Christie, Marshall, & Lanthier, 1977, cited in Murphy, Coleman, & Abel, 1983) although distributions of IQ scores tend to skew toward the lower end (Mohr, Turner, & Jerry, 1964; MacDonald, 1973; Brown and Courtless, 1968; Langevin, 1984; Stokes, 1964).

Some of the earlier prevalence studies have been biased by the inclusion of "sex offences" such as "urinating in a public place" (Hall, 1974). In fact there are numerous cases cited in the literature and by professionals working in the area in which the offence committed is one which could have been prevented simply by the presentation of sexual information and education on private vs. public acts. This kind of behavior may be a particular problem for institutionalized individuals as they would have been less likely to receive appropriate education. It is clear that these are not offences which can be put in the same category with offences such as child molestation and sexual assault. This distinction should be made clear to social workers, police officers, and the court system.

It must be acknowledged that a large number of offences committed by individuals with intellectual impairments are not of this "naive" variety. This point has been stressed by several professionals who work with offenders (Udell, 07/87; Eakin, 07/87; Hyman, 07/87). In the following discussion of sex offences only those offences which could realistically be put into the category of child sexual assault or molestation will be considered.

Several authors have stressed that this slight overrepresentation of the offender who has been labelled mentally retarded may well represent the lower social skills and cognitive abilities of the individual with a disability which makes them more likely to be caught than the offender without such impairments (Murphy, Coleman, & Abel, 1982; Santamour & West, 1978; Murphy, Coleman, & Haynes, 1983). For example, Virkkunen (1974) has suggested the incest offender with an intellectual impairment may be less adept at keeping the secret.

For the purposes of this discussion it is assumed that individuals with developmental disabilities are no more or less likely to sexually abuse children than other people. When they do however, issues of treatment and handling in the criminal justic system are complicated by the presence of the disability.

Sex Offenders with Intellectual Impairments in the Criminal Justice System

The handling of the offender with a developmental disability may differ substantially from the handling of other offenders. Brown and Courtless (1968) reviewed the course of criminal justice for the offender labelled mentally retarded in all types of crime and found: 1) that confessions or incriminating statements were obtained in two thirds of the cases, 2) offenders were usually defended by a court appointed lawyer with eight percent having no lawyer at all, 3) unlike the cases of other offenders, the offender labelled mentally retarded rarely had charges against him lowered once they had been laid, 4) in most cases no psychological or psychiatric examination was conducted nor was competency to stand trial discussed, and 5) in 88 percent of the cases no appeal was filed. Santamour and West (1978) more recently compared defendants with intellectual impairments with non-disabled defendants and found that those with developmental disabilities more often plead guilty or confessed while there were fewer plea bargains or appealed convictions. They were also given probation and parole less frequently. While the court system has protected alleged perpetrators from the testimony of children with developmental disabilities quite effectively (see section on testimony of children), it seems less prone to protect the alleged perpetrator with a disability from the legal system itself.

The flip side of the situation in which an alleged offender receives inadequate protection of his rights is suggested by Batya Hyman, a therapist who has assessed over 50 sex offenders with intellectual impairments. She suggests that in some cases the offender with a developmental disability is actually protected from legal remedies by the agencies with which he is affiliated. She gave the example of the Department of Mental Health in her state stepping in and agreeing to provide 24 hour supervision for an offender in lieu of sentencing. Some example of more lenient treatment for child molesters with intellectual impairments can be found in case studies presented in the Badgley report. In one instance of incestuous assault on the offender's five-year-old daughter, the appeal "court stated that it would have been more severe in sentencing but for the accused's low intelligence, personality defects and progress toward rehabilitation since being sentenced" (p. 874). In another case, "the attempted rape of a two-year-old girl", "The Court of Appeal ruled that in spite of the gravity of the offence, which necessitated a substantial prison term as a general deterrent, the accused was considered to be harmless and dull-witted, and had no prior history indicating a predisposition toward violent or sexually assaultive behavior. It was also felt that the accused was unlikely to derive much benefit from imprisonment. Furthermore, although the victim was young, she had suffered no serious physical or psychological harm as a result of the offence" (p. 876). It helps no one to have one set of rules for the population not shown to have intellectual impairments and another for those who happen to have a developmental disability. While humane treatment should be guaranteed, special lenience is not called for.

Once individuals with intellectual impairments have been convicted of sexually abusing a child, problems arise with placement. Historically, the incarceration of offenders labelled mentally retarded in the existing prisons was seen to be a problem, particularly since it was assumed that the criminality was based on the hereditary intellectual impairment (Brown & Courtless, 1968). On the other hand, the seclusion of offenders to institutions meant for non-offending individuals labelled mentally retarded was also a problem as they were perceived to be a bad influence. The solution proposed was a separate system and a plan which included two features, sterilization and, colonization and segregation (Goddard, 1912, cited in Brown & Courtless, 1968). Brown and Courtless summarized the international situation in 1968. Countries such as England and Sweden seemed most concerned about the therapeutic and treatment interventions which could be provided in the setting and therefore tended to house "defective delinquents" with "non-delinquent defectives". The North American focus on the other hand was on "security and custodial care" (p. 364) so individuals labelled mentally retarded were more likely to be incarcerated in prisons or mental hospitals.

The situation has not changed dramatically since that time. In a more recent survey of facilities for people labelled mentally retarded (Coleman & Murphy, 1980) 15 percent of the facilities "reported an average of three sex offenders (i.e., rapists, child molesters, etc.) in their patient population" (p. 272). Only one fifth of these institutions had treatment programs for the sex offenders, and very few of the total number of facilities knew of treatment programs in their states. When treatment programs are not offered, difficulties arise. "Compared to residents in facilities for the retarded, offenders tend to be at the higher end of the range of functioning and often manipulate and victimize those who function at lower levels" (Murphy, Coleman, & Haynes, 1983, p. 26). Thus the facility is presented with issues it was never prepared for nor equipped to handle.

Murphy, Coleman and Haynes (1983) reported that in their experience, prisons and in-patient psychiatric facilities were most often used to confine offenders with intellectual impairments. While these settings *may* be more likely to offer treatment than the institutions for non-offending individuals there is no guarantee that the sex offender with a developmental disability will be included in the treatment program. Further, there is evidence that offenders with intellectual impairments "in prison or in a correctional program tend to function at the bottom of the intelligence range of that population and [are] often victimized by other offenders" (Murphy, Coleman, & Haynes, 1983, p. 26). The same problem appears to exist in Canada with some documentation of the increased victimization of men with intellectual impairments in the prison system (Makin, 1987). Sex offenders with mental handicaps also have been known to victimize "acutely psychotic patients" in inpatient facilities (Murphy, Coleman, & Haynes, 1983). Clearly, the current system is not working if the sex offender with a developmental disability is not receiving treatment to prevent further offending, is being sexually abused himself while incarcerated, or is continuing to abuse others sexually.

Coleman, Murphy, and Haynes (1983) who are among the few psychologists who will treat sex offenders with developmental disabilities suggest that "the optimal solution would probably be a specialized treatment program for mentally retarded sex offenders in which individuals have similar intellectual levels" (p. 26-27) in an outpatient setting for those who would benefit; and with strict restrictions placed on offender behavior in residential facilities for those offenders who are deemed too dangerous to be released. For a good discussion of treatment settings and how to assess risks to the community for all sex offenders, see Knopp (1984).

The inadequacies of the current system for convictions and treatment of sex offenders are well documented in the Badgley report (1984). Most sex offenders in Canada do not receive treatment of any kind. The Badgley report does not mention the offender with intellectual impairments explicitly however it can be presumed from the research reviewed that the situation for this population of offenders is at least as severe.

Treatment Issues

The inaccessibility of treatment programs appears to be as much of a problem for the offender with a developmental disability as it is for victims with the disability. Many of the same issues apply. Knopp, Rosenberg and Stevenson (1986) performed a nationwide survey of programs offered for sex-offenders. They reported that only 46 percent of the services available served offenders with developmental disabilities in any way, and only 26 percent of those services had made special adaptations for the offenders with developmental disabilities. Empirical evidence is not available and clinical observations not published as to the applicability of programs to the offender with an intellectual impairment. It may be therefore that professionals running treatment programs do not know if their service is appropriate for the offender with a developmental disability. This leaves the field in a state of hit and miss. Some programs exclude offenders with developmental disabilities altogether (as do many treatment programs for adolescent offenders in Metro Toronto (Udell, 07/87)); some accept offenders with developmental disabilities but do not feel that they are served well by the program (Barbaree, 06/87); while others accept them and find that existing methods of treatment work well with only minor adaptations (Murphy, Cole, & Haynes, 1983; Hyman, 07/87). Studies of the effectiveness of treatment programs for the offender with intellectual impairments are required.

The model of treatment presented by Coleman, Murphy and Haynes (1982) is the same for offenders with and without disabilities. The differences are in the emphasis and mode of presentation. This model is reproduced in Figure 11. It is a social learning model which includes physiological, behavioral, and cognitive processes and deficits. The program is tailored for the individual in question. As Coleman, Murphy, and Haynes (1982) stress, "Individuals who have the same IQs may be quite different in their social functioning, social knowledge, and insight into their behavioral problems." (p. 25) They recognize that offenders who have grown up in institutional settings will differ considerably from offenders who have been socialized in their own homes, for instance. These authors also point out that just as many non-disabled offenders have more problems than simply their sexual exploitation of children, offenders with developmental disabilities may also have psychiatric problems, other behavior disorders, or deficits such as speech impairments. They stress that treatment programs must address the specific needs of the individual to be effective.

Special issues involved in the treatment of sex offenders with developmental disabilities. Marshall, Barbaree and Christophe (1986) have assessed many child molesters and incest perpetrators in Ontario. Their results have some possible implications for the handling and treatment of offenders with intellectual impairments. Among the sample of men they assessed were a number of men with "low IQ's" as judged by performance on Raven's Progressive Matrices Test. When the data from men with "low IQ's" were examined separately it was found that, 1) the child molesters were more aroused to children than the molesters with higher IQ's and, 2) men in both the incest offenders and non-offenders ("normals") groups were more likely to "display deviant sexual interests at assessment" (p. 436). Arousal does not predict that they will act on their attraction. However, these authors suggest that either "appropriate constraints against arousal to young girls" (p.436) have been learned or there is some problem with age discrimination. They support the latter explanation. It is also possible that men with intellectual impairments are less able than other men to control their erections in the experimental setting. Further research is required before any conclusions can be drawn.

Two issues in the model in Figure 11, social skills and sexual knowledge and education have been documented to be particular trouble spots for offenders with intellectual impairments (Murphy, Cole & Haynes, 1983). As has been documented earlier, many children with developmental disabilities do not receive sex education or assertiveness training. Lack of information may be a risk factor both for the likelihood of being abused and the likelihood of abusing. Udell (07/87) has noted that the adolescent offenders with developmental disabilities he has seen do not lack sex education of the "plumbing" variety, but rather lack information about sexual relationships and sexuality. Most sex offenders have deficits in these two areas but it seems that they are even more severe for the offender with a developmental disability.

Another issue which must be addressed is the suggestion that a large number of offenders were themselves victimized as children. "What we are finding as a prominent influence in the life histories of sexual offenders is their own experience of sexual victimization as children, and this discovery has influenced our thinking in how to help offenders" (Groth, 1983, cited in Knopp, 1984, p. 38). It has been shown previously that boys with intellectual impairments are likely at higher risk for sexual abuse. If prior sexual victimization is a factor in offending behavior then the boy with a developmental disability would also be at risk for developing abusive coping mechanisms. Griffiths (06/87) at the York Behavioral Management Program stated that 100 percent of the offenders with developmental disabilities she had currently in the program had been sexually abused as children. Clearly, prevention efforts must also address their role in the prevention of abuse in the next generation.

One of the important features of the treatment program is the setting in which it is offered. Coleman, Murphy and Haynes (1982) have experience primarily with an outpatient setting. The treatment model used in Kingston, Ontario by Marshall and Barbaree[15] is also primarily on an outpatient basis. Coleman, Murphy and Haynes (1983) have stressed the importance of family cooperation for the effective treatment of the offender with an intellectual impairment.

It is worth reproducing their warning here that some families may attempt to use the therapist to have the family member/offender institutionalized. This is not a desirable outcome of the therapy process and must be avoided.

Treatments to correct the offender's inappropriate arousal to children are largely aversive in nature and for this reason there are serious ethical concerns with their implementation. Critiques of these methods are many, on ethical and other grounds, as are the professionals suggesting that these methods are the only ones with a proven success rate. A discussion of the methods used is beyond the scope of this report. They are summarized elsewhere (Langevin, 1983; Badgley et al., 1984; Knopp, 1984; and in Figure 11). The Badgley report (1984) has made the situation very clear with regard to the effectiveness of correctional treatment programs. They state: "The consensus of numerous reviews of the operation of correctional treatment programs for convicted sexual offenders suggest that there is insufficient evidence available either to warrant the conclusion "that nothing works" or the optimism that certain programs have been "demonstrably successful" " (p. 880). This author supports Coleman et al.'s position that the least intrusive method possible should be used and only with the informed consent of the offender (which rules out some offenders). This policy would guarantee the offender with an intellectual impairment the best possible treatment without violating their rights.

Adolescent Sex Offenders.　Adolescent sex offenders with mental handicaps have even less access to services and treatment programs than their adult counterparts. In the Knopp, Rosenberg and Stevenson (1986) survey, only 16 percent of the services available to adolescent sex offenders were available to adolescents with developmental disabilities. Udell (07/87) has recently conducted research in the metro Toronto area (research as yet unpublished) establishing that there are very limited services available for these offenders. Many services which deal specifically with adolescent sex offenders have a policy of not taking the offenders with intellectual impairments. Considering that most sex offenders begin their illegal activities while they are adolescents, and that there are increasing numbers of adolescent offenders (Mathews, undated), the need for services and treatment for this population is urgent if sexual abuse is to be prevented.

9

LEGAL ISSUES IN
SEXUAL ABUSE OF CHILDREN

Consent

Individuals with developmental disabilities have historically been prohibited from engaging in consensual sexual activity, due to the assumption that the presence of the disability meant an inherent inability to consent (Kempton, 1977; Greenland, 1983). This practice could lead to the arrest of any male partner of a woman with an intellectual impairment for rape. The practice of denying sexual rights to individuals with mental handicaps has been questioned in the past two decades with the more recent position on sexuality being one of "normalization" (Kempton, 1977; Turnbull, 1977). In Canada, the law which restricted women with developmental disabilities from consensual sexual activity (Section 148) was repealed in 1983. A discussion of the sexual rights of adults with mental handicaps is well beyond the scope of this report. An acknowledgement of the historical precedent in this field is necessary however, to ensure that in the task of protecting children with developmental disabilities from sexual abuse and exploitation, one does not also "protect" adolescents and adults with disabilities from healthy sexual expression.

With consent, as with other issues, "no universally applicable standards can be applied to the mentally handicapped since they do not constitute a cohesive, consistent, or definable group" (Rioux, 1979, p. 76). People working with sexually abused individuals with intellectual impairments have stressed the importance of assessing ability to consent on an individual basis (Aguilar, 1984; Baladerian, 1985b; Blomberg, undated).

The Criminal Code of Canada, as amended in January 1988, assumes that *all* children under the age of 14 cannot give consent to sexual activity with an adult. There is no reason the issue of consent should be different for children with mental handicaps under 14 years of age.

Issues of consent arise specifically for adolescents with developmental disabilities when they are over 14 years of age at which time the law allows consent as a defense. It must be remembered that the issue of consent would arise primarily in circumstances of no physical harm, no complaint by the alleged victim, or a non-verbal victim, and the concern of other adults that the adolescent had in fact been exploited. Consent would not (hopefully) be the primary issue in a case of forced sexual assault with a complaint by the victim and evidence of harm, although the 1983 amendments to the law made this possible (Badgley et al, 1984).

The American Penal Code defines consent to be "positive cooperation in act or attitude pursuant to an exercise of free will. The persons must act freely and voluntarily and have knowledge of the nature of the act or transaction involved." (cited in Baladerian, 1985, p. 3).[16] There are three elements that must be taken into account to determine whether legally valid consent has been given (Blomberg, undated; Rioux, 1979; Turnbull, 1977; Dillon, 1980). First, the consent must be voluntary with no coercion, intimidation, or pressure present. Turnbull (1977) has discussed the problems that may arise with voluntary consent when an individual is institutionalized, is dependent on someone for care, is inexperienced or cannot seek outside advice. The provisions contained in the recent amendments to Criminal Code will, in theory, help to alleviate this problem by prohibiting all sexual contact between a young person and someone in a position of trust. The second element in consent is informational, requiring that a person have the information necessary to make a decision. Blomberg's (undated) view is that an individual who has not gone through the developmental stage which enables them to say "no" to a request, cannot be considered to have had the information available to them to say "yes". It could also be argued that individuals who have had no access to sex education would not have the information necessary to consent to sexual activity.[17] The third element is that the person must have the capability to give consent. Blomberg (undated) summarized capability by stating that "a person is competent to consent validly if she/he fully appreciates the nature and consequences of the matter in question" (p. 2). It is crucial that competency to consent to sexual activity be assessed specifically and not inferred from the individual's ability to perform unrelated tasks or to remember unrelated information (Blomberg, undated; Baladerian, 1985). Baladerian (1985) in particular is concerned that judgements of ability to consent not be made by uninformed persons based on IQ scores or knowledge of unrelated topics.

A well utilized standardized measure would help immensely in this difficult area. Blomberg (1987) has created an instrument for assessing an individual's sexual knowledge. It has been adapted from the EASE (Essential Adult Sex Education) instrument developed by Zelman (1976, cited in Blomberg, 1987) and is supplemented with a structured interview and play technique. It was originally developed as an evaluation tool to test the effectiveness of prevention programs but is currently being tested further in the hope that it will be able to stand up in court as a measure of competency. This is a valid instrument with good potential. Expert witnesses who have had experience both with developmental disabilities *and* sexual issues should also be found to assist with decisions about the ability of an individual to consent.

Ability to Testify

Non-verbal Victims. Very young children and children with severe disabilities often lack verbal skills. Pre-verbal and non-verbal children under the age of 14 are protected under the law against sexual abuse but may be unable to communicate the abuse. "In the case of the pre-verbal child who has been molested, another witness or corroborating evidence would be necessary in pursuing prosecution" (Stevens & Berliner, 1980, p. 249). It has been documented that the impact of sexual abuse on pre-verbal children is still dramatic. One study has shown that once children gain the verbal skills necessary, they can accurately report what had happened to them before, even without prompting or rehearsal (cited in Jones & McQuiston, 1984).

Non-verbal adolescents and adolescents with limited verbal ability would not be able to testify under normal circumstances unless they were able to communicate via a bliss board or sign language. It is possible that some children would be able to tell a court what happened to them if they were able to use an interpreter who was familiar with their speech patterns. A ruling of the admissibility of an interpreter for other than foreign languages or sign language would have to be made for this to be possible (Endicott, 07/87).

Verbal victims.   Ability to legally consent to sexual activity is a different standard of competency by definition than the competency to testify. Most authors have distinguished between these capacities (Aguilar, 1984; Baladerian, 1985). In child sexual abuse cases, the capacity of the child to testify or to be a competent witness is questioned for most children especially young ones. The differential impact of the law on children with intellectual impairments is evident because their ability to testify is questioned at a much older chronological age simply because of their disability. Until very recently in Canadian common law, five components of competency needed to be fulfilled for any person to testify. They were that the person: 1) "has sufficient intelligence to make it worthwhile to hear him or her at all"; 2) "had the capacity at the time of the events in question to observe them"; 3) "has the capacity to recall the events in question"; 4) has the capacity to narrate the events in question"; and 5) "feels a duty to tell the truth" (McKague, 1985, p. 19). One exception to these rules for children was found in Section 16 of the Evidence Act which allowed a young child to give evidence without having been sworn "provided that 'the child is possessed of sufficient intelligence to justify the reception of the evidence, and understands the duty of speaking the truth' " (Endicott, 1987, p. 23). This evidence then had to be corroborated. These strict rules of competency have ruled out the testimony of young children with average intelligence (Poirier, 1986) as well as the evidence of adults with developmental disabilities who were considered unable to give sworn evidence (CACL, 1986). Thus the likelihood that a child with a developmental disability would be able to testify in a sexual abuse situation (in which corroborating evidence is seldom available) was virtually impossible under the current laws. The testimony of adolescents with developmental disabilities might have been considered if they were ruled to be of "tender years" as well as "of sufficient intelligence" *and* there was corroborating evidence. It is not surprising therefore that virtually no cases of sexual assault or child sexual abuse against a victim with a developmental disability went forward or was successful since the 1983 law prohibiting sexual intercourse with a "feeble-minded female" was changed.[18]

The same Act of Parliament (Bill C-15) which amended the Criminal Code in January 1988 also introduced significant changes in the Canada Evidence Act. These amendments alter the competency requirements in a way that may allow children and adolescents with developmental disabilities more access to the judicial process. The revisions change the "sufficient intelligence" clause to one in which the person's "ability to communicate" becomes the test. Further, if the court finds the person lacks an understanding of "the nature of an oath or a solemn affirmation," he or she may be permitted to testify "on promising to tell the truth." The requirement that the unsworn person's testimony be corroborated has also been removed. These changes, in combination with Section 6 of the Canada Evidence Act, which provides for the possibility of non-verbal communication, and the use of an interpreter, could result in progressive law. Children and adolescents with intellectual impairments could, with proper support and assistance, be given the opportunity to testify about their victimization.[19] Changes to the Criminal Code also place the burden of proof of incompetence of an adolescent over 14 onto the party who challenges the mental capacity of the proposed witness.

These changes in the Evidence Act redirect the focus from the child's ability to testify at all to the ability of the child to give intelligible and credible testimony. This puts all children and adolescents (regardless of age or intellectual abilities) onto more equal footing.

Once the ability of a child or adolescent to promise to tell the truth and to communicate what has occurred has been established, issues of ability to observe and recall events come to the surface.

Credibility of the Child's Testimony

Canadian laws with regard to children's testimony assume that children are less credible than adults. This assumption was based on research done and theories of memory held by Binet and others in the early 1900's (Lefkowitz, 06/87). Memory was thought to follow an orderly developmental progression, from the newborn state of no memory to the adult state with memory in its full capacity. It has been shown more recently that processes in memory develop at different times and there are differences in the development of these processes and their ability to function between individuals and within an individual over different situations (Jones & McQuiston, 1984). Thus no universal conclusions can be made about children's memories. Similarly, children with intellectual impairments will vary in their ability to observe, process, and recall information. A brief review of the literature on the abilities of children to give credible evidence will now be presented.[20]

Free recall.   In a situation of free recall, (where the child is asked what happened in an open ended manner) children produce fewer details and less overall information than adults, with the least information produced by very young children (Lefkowitz, 06/87; Goodman & Reed, 1984, cited in Goodman & Helgeson, 1985; Marin, Holmes, Guth & Kovac, 1979). The information they do give, however, appears to be quite accurate (Fivush, 1984, cited in Goodman & Helgeson, 1985; Lefkowitz, 06/87; Johnson & Foley, 1984). It has been suggested that children give less information in these situations because they have less information of the world and have a less complex view of it than adults (Lefkowitz, 06/87; Jones & McQuiston, 1984). It may also be possible that the problem arises from the child's inability to find the language to express what the child does know (Jones & McQuiston, 1984). The only exception to this situation would occur when a child had more knowledge and familiarity with a situation than the adult. In this case the child would likely be *more* accurate than the adult (Chi, 1978).

Forgetting.   Both adults and children forget events over time. This is the reason that witness statements must be given as soon as possible after an event. Ability to remember in adults has been shown to be affected by: the amount of stress and the relevance of the material to the person over time (Jones & McQuiston, 1984); whether the details are of central importance to the person (Marquis, Marshall & Oskamp, 1972); and the length of time over which the event occurred (Dent & Stephenson, 1979).

The research on the memory of children has found similar variations with the most accurate and detailed memory being for: details which were central rather than peripheral[21] (Marquis, Marshall & Oskamp, 1972; Goodman & Reed, 1984, cited in Goodman & Helgeson, 1985), events which occurred over an extended period of time (Goodman & Reed, 1984, cited in Goodman & Helgeson, 1985; Dent & Stephenson, 1979), events which were repeated (Fivush, 1984, cited in Goodman & Helgeson; Sanders & Warnick, 1981), and situations in which the perpetrator was known to the victim (Bahrick, Bahrick & Wittlinger, 1975). These strengths and limitations of memory and forgetting must be remembered when a child victim is being questioned.

Hard (05/87) has been able to verify (through access to medical records) that adults with developmental disabilities accurately recalled sexual abuse including the timing of the abuse as many as eight or nine years later. She asserts that individuals with developmental disabilities can remember when an event has happened.

Temporal order of events. Temporal order of events is seen by some authors to be the most serious problem encountered in a child's memory (Singer & Reveson, 1978; de Young, 1986). This has been empirically established only for events of peripheral importance to the child (Jones & McQuiston, 1984; Lefkowitz, 06/87). Lefkowitz (06/87) has suggested that asking the child to remember by relating the event to other events which are of importance[22] is a useful way to assist a child's memory. It is stressed that incorrect recall of the order of events does not imply that other details are also incorrect (Goodman & Helgeson, 1985).

Some professionals working with individuals with developmental disabilities have suggested that ordering events is a problem for them also (Stigall, 20/05/87) but can sometimes be remedied by gently probing for time information.

Children (regardless of level of impairment) should not be expected always to recall dates and times of events. Defense attorneys who insist on using these kinds of questions to discredit child witnesses should be educated about the inappropriateness of their requests and another line of questioning suggested.

Suggestibility. The area in which the most general concern has been expressed about the testimony of children has been in the area of suggestibility. Adults have been shown to be affected by leading questions and interviewing techniques and they are particularly suggestible in eyewitness recognition of perpetrators (Loftus, 1979). Children have also been found to be suggestible (Jones & McQuiston, 1984, Lefkowitz, 06/87) but again more with regard to peripheral events than central details. Goodman, Hirschman and Rudy (1987) have shown experimentally that children are quite resistant to leading questions when they have experienced rather than witnessed the event, the event was stressful, and the questions were specific to an abuse situation. Younger children were more suggestible than older children but were still quite resistant to leading questions about the central event. These authors suggest that former research on the suggestibility of children has been misleading since it had little ecological validity, usually questioning children about witnessed rather than experienced events, asking them questions about a nonstressful event, as well as asking them questions which would have no relevance to an abuse investigation.

There are many reasons not to ask children leading questions; only one of which is people's fear of their suggestibility (Jones & McQuiston, 1984; Croezen, 06/87). There has been no research conducted which can verify the extent of suggestibility in victims with developmental disabilities Eakin (07/87) has suggested that leading questions may be necessary with some adolescents with intellectual impairments to get the information required. It would be wise to use a non-leading style with all children whenever it is possible. Video-taping of the interview also helps to show that leading questions were not used (or prove that they were, for that matter). Individual assessment of the suggestibility of the individual is also possible in a clinical setting (Jones & McQuiston, 1984).

Other factors affecting memory. Authority figures and intimidating surroundings have been shown to decrease the individual's ability to remember events (Dent & Stephenson, 1979) and to increase the effect of leading questions (Ceci, Ross & Toglia, 1985 cited in Goodman & Helgeson, 1985). Child victims are more likely to be intimidated by an interview with an adult authority figure than adult victims (Croezen, 06/87). Croezen (06/87) stresses that many children need to be assured that they are not in trouble. In a situation in which the child is being interviewed in a police station or other such setting, intimidation could be expected to be extreme. For children with developmental disabilities this may be even more stressful. As has been shown previously, their training has often included the teaching of blind trust and obedience to adults.

There is no straightforward relationship between intellectual impairment and memory. Individuals process, remember and communicate information more or less well, depending on numerous variables involved in the situation and the individual. It is possible to assess these on an individual basis. Blomberg (undated) has produced a list of cognitive skills which she believes may be impaired in some individuals with developmental disabilities. She suggests that the presence of these cognitive skills should be assessed on an individual basis (See Figure 10). The interviewer can then act to reduce or alleviate many of these problems by using alternative types of questions, play and interview techniques. See Jones and McQuiston (1984), Blomberg (undated), Baladerian (1985), Goodman and Helgeson (1985), and Stevens and Berliner (1980) for more detailed information about the investigative interview.

It was once assumed that children's testimony was less credible than adults. This has found only limited support in the new research on child witnesses. While children may have deficits in memory processes this is not uniform or predictable. Moreover, many of these deficits can be overcome to some extent by the use of careful questioning and the use of props and toys to trigger memory. Children with intellectual impairments will also vary in terms of their ability to process and recall information, with no uniformity or predictability based on their age or degree of impairment. In all children it is more likely that they will remember central details, events which occurred over a long time or were repeated, and acts which were committed by a known adult. Consequently, a child witness is likely to perform best when testifying about the average sexual abuse situation.

The difference between the *ability* to perform the tasks required and the *credibility* of the evidence produced by those tasks is stressed in a statement from the California Supreme Court: "It bears emphasis that the witness' competency depends upon his ability to perceive, recollect, and communicate. Whether he did perceive accurately, does recollect, and is communicating accurately and truthfully are questions of credibility to be resolved by the trier of fact." (cited in Aguilar, 1984, p. 11). Once it is established that the child has the ability to observe, recall and communicate what has happened to her, her credibility will be assessed by the judge or jury. In order that their judgements be based upon the evidence of the child and not on misconceptions about children's testimony in general or beliefs about the capacities of individuals with developmental disabilities in general, juries should be selected with these issues in mind and judges educated about the issues involved.

The new child sexual abuse law: The impact on children with developmental disabilities

Bill C-15 went through its third and final reading in the summer of 1987 and was proclaimed in January 1988. It is too early yet to tell how it will be used in practice. Theoretically, the provisions in the new law which deal with child sexual abuse will benefit all children.

Such benefits include the removal of gender specific crimes in which the accused must be male and the victim female (former Sections 146(1), 146(2), 147, 151, 152, 153(1), 154), particularly so that male victims are equally protected under the law. Inclusion represents the specific types of sexual touching and invitation to touch which are most likely to occur in sexual abuse rather than a strict focus on genital intercourse (new Sections 141, 146), is also an improvement. The removal of the requirement of "previous chaste character" for female victims between 14 and 16, and the notion that an adolescent might be "more to blame" for an abusive incident (allowing her sexual history to be entered as evidence) have modernized the law. The removal of the one-year time limit is also beneficial. All of these changes were recommendations of the Badgley report and have created a law which more accurately represents the realities of the sexual abuse situation.

A further benefit of the sexual exploitation charge is that it proceeds in a summary fashion which involves a shorter time from the start of the court process to its conclusion (Hallet, 06/87). The new law also means that perpetrators convicted of these offences will be easily recognized as child exploiters. Prior to 1988, convictions such as "gross indecency" did not clearly identify the crime as one against a child.

The use of videotaping and the removal of the alleged perpetrator from the victim's view[23] will affect all children in much the same way. It makes the court system a more humane experience, with less stress associated with it. Several articles have recently been written on the correct management of videotaped interviews. These should be consulted (Colby & Colby, 1987; Stevens & Berliner, 1980) and supplemented with general information available on the interview techniques mentioned earlier.

The revision in the sexual abuse legislation which is of the most significant assistance to the child or adolescent with a mental handicap is the repeal of the current Sections 146 and 147 and their replacement with the sexual exploitation drafting. It has been shown that the child with an intellectual impairment is more likely than other children to be abused by a known individual (Hard, 1987; Ryerson, 1984) who is in a position of trust. However, the relationship may not involve a blood relation (Section 150) or a foster father, stepfather, or employer (former Section 153(1)). Furthermore, the sexual activity involved is not always completed sexual intercourse. The Criminal Code now prohibits a wider range of sexual activities.

Changes in the Evidence Act could bring about the greatest changes in access to the legal system for the child or adolescent with a mental handicap. Ontario Crown attorney Shelley Hallet (06/87) believes these new laws would make the child with a developmental disability a more easily acceptable witness. She also stressed that, in her experience, when a child is judged able to testify, especially in the case of younger children, the perpetrator often changes his plea to guilty. Most charges of sexual offences against children do in fact usually result in guilty pleas (Hallet, 06/87). A guilty plea protects the child from actually having to testify.

Until very recently, children and adolescents with intellectual impairments have no access to the legal system. They were rarely if ever judged able to testify about their abuse. With little or no corroborating evidence likely, the Crown would not take cases involving witnesses with intellectual impairments to court. While all children's rights were abridged, and few perpetrators brought up on charges, the child with a disability was even further denied. In theory, recent revisions to the law are a great improvement in the legal situation for children with and without disabilities. In practice it remains to be seen whether society is ready to make the strong statement that children and adolescents with intellectual impairments are *not* perfect victims.

RECOMMENDATIONS

This report has documented the existence of victims of child sexual abuse with intellectual impairments. In fact, it has been suggested that the presence of a developmental disability may indirectly and directly create a situation in which the child with the disability is put at higher risk for sexual abuse. Many of the contributing factors to this increased vulnerability are created by the education and conditioning that a child with an intellectual impairment experiences. Others are the result of attitudes in the society which make the child with a developmental disability a more acceptable victim. Changes can and need to be made in both of these areas. It must be noted that sexual abuse and exploitation of individuals with intellectual impairments is not restricted to those under 18 years of age. Many cases of sexual assault and exploitation against adults with developmental disabilities came to light during the course of this research. Future studies should address this population more specifically.

While sexual abuse occurs in institutional settings, it also occurs in group homes, foster homes, and in families of origin. With the current trend toward deinstitutionalization the need for services in the community to address the needs of the sexually victimized child will be increased.

Tragically, when the child with a mental handicap has been victimized, the services available to her are extremely limited. She will probably receive medical attention if she is taken to a hospital or clinic, but for the many children who see only visiting physicians, medical attention for the abuse is not guaranteed. When a report is made to provincial child protective services, the workers have not had much experience dealing with children with developmental disabilities, and may be unable or unwilling to give the child full services. For example, they may think that the use of anatomically correct dolls in an interview with a fifteen-year-old boy is inappropriate, when in fact that is what is needed in the individual case (Eakin, 07/87). Both the child and staff in facilities for individuals with developmental disabilities would be unlikely to know which services were available and accessible to child victims with disabilities. Since fairly specialized counselling is required for victims of sexual abuse, the child would be unlikely to get the help she needs.

If the abuse happened in the child's own home, she may be removed to a foster home, group home or institution, where she is at high risk for further sexual abuse. If the abuse occurred in an institution or other facility, the abuse may be dealt with internally in which case the offender might be believed, warned, or dismissed. The victim is often not informed about the process and is expected to get over the abuse, either on her own or with the help of personnel with little or no training. The offense is rarely reported to the police and of those cases which are, very few offenders will be apprehended and charged. Under the current laws and with limited corroborating evidence, a crown attorney would not be able to put the child with an intellectual impairment on the stand in most cases, and would therefore ask that charges be dropped.

In the case of a perpetrator with a developmental disability, the situation is similarly tragic. The legal system was not designed to accommodate the needs of the person with an intellectual impairment and it often fails them. The prison systems were designed to punish offenders and they have trouble providing the treatment and services necessary to prevent sex offenders from offending again. In addition, the few services that exist were not intended or designed to accommodate the offender with a developmental disability.

Changes to be effective must occur on several different fronts and must not be superficial. The following recommendations give suggestions as to the source and the direction necessary for change to be effected.

1. **PREVENTION**

   "Quick fixes" must be avoided. Prevention programs should be well thought out, planned, carried out, and then evaluated to ensure their effectiveness. Prevention programming should not be aimed restrictively at children but rather should include efforts directed at children, parents, professionals (such as doctors, nurses, social workers, psychologists), and institutional management and staff.

   a. **Children**
      i. Sex education must become a normal part of every child's life at a very early age. This education cannot simply include anatomical information but must address sexual rights and responsibilities as are appropriate to the child's age and level of development. Sex education programs must not simply be assumed to be effective. Evaluation should be an integral part of the sex education program. These programs should not be a "one shot" affair, but rather integrated into the education of the child over time.
      ii. Physical self-protection skills should be considered a part of every child's physical education. Sexual abuse prevention programs vary dramatically and should be selected carefully with regard to their approach, philosophies, method of teaching, effectiveness, and reputation. Children should all be taught "avoidance, resistance, and help seeking techniques" (Finkelhor & Araji, 1983, p. 14). Sexual abuse prevention programs can be worked into the education program that children are already engaged in. The fact that a child lives in a residential facility should only further guarantee that these programs are offered. It cannot be assumed that children are receiving this information at home, or in their current school system.
      iii. The environments which house and educate children must be designed or renovated to include the facilities necessary for the child to report abuse. Access to a private phone should be considered a right. Privacy should be guaranteed as an important part of any child's (or adult's) living situation.

   b. **Parents**
      The increased interest which parents of children with developmental disabilities seem to be showing with regard to sexual education and sexual abuse prevention should be encouraged. Prevention programs should be set up for parents (most

beneficially in co-ordination with the programs offered to children) which cover the topics: sexual information, sexual abuse prevention, and recognition of the signs and symptoms of abuse. Parents must be taught that their children may be at higher risk for abuse at the same time that they are taught how to deal constructively with their fears.

c. **Professionals**

All professionals who are in contact with children with intellectual impairments should be trained to deal (minimally on a crisis intervention level) with sexual abuse. As Sgroi (1975) stressed, the fact that a professional believes that the abuse is possible increases the likelihood that they will diagnose and respond to the sexual abuse. Specialization of some professionals within a system may be required, however, all professionals should know: how to recognize the signs and symptoms of abuse, how to respond to a disclosure, and what referrals to make. Education of the medical personnel who are responsible for health care in institutional facilities is particularly urgent.

d. **Institutions**[24]

i. Sex education and sexual abuse prevention programming must be provided in all institutional facilities. Again, the programs should be carefully chosen, planned, implemented, and evaluated. These should be an integral part of the programming in the facility. The environment in the facility should reinforce not contradict the messages which have been taught in these courses. Commitment at all levels of the institutional hierarchy to these ideals is a necessary part of the prevention program. Education must occur to ensure this commitment. Staff, parents, and residents should be included in the planning stages of the programs to ensure that implementation is successful. The programs should be taught by knowledgeable individuals who are comfortable with the issues involved. If such a person is not available within the current structure, a person or persons from outside the facility are required.

ii. Screening of employees should be carried out with the knowledge that few if any sex offenders will be screened out by the procedure.

iii. Committees should be formed immediately to establish ethical policies covering two main areas; sexual activity between residents in the facility and contact between staff and residents.

These policies should be widely distributed. Staff interactions with residents should be guided by the knowledge of appropriate treatment techniques and handling of residents especially those who have been previously abused. Training sessions will be necessary in many cases to ensure this. Protocols for dealing with allegations of sexual abuse must be established explicitly. All allegations which would fall under the definition of sexual abuse should be reported and then investigated and dealt with externally. Residents and their parents must be protected against retaliation from the institutional management, staff or other residents in the event that they have made a report of sexual abuse.

iv. The work environments of institutional facilities should be humanized in an effort to reduce stress on personnel.

2. SERVICE PROVISION/AGENCIES

a. "Real" Accessibility

The minimum level of accessibility of services acceptable is "real" accessibility. This means that the child victim with an intellectual impairment would be helped in a meaningful way by any service agency which normally serves the victims of sexual abuse. Government funding for the education and training of agency staff and other service providers may be required. Service providers and agencies whose mandate is the individual with a developmental disability must also be trained to deal (minimally on a crisis management basis) with the sexual abuse victim. Networking, liaising, and mutual education between agencies which serve primarily victims of sexual abuse and those which serve individuals with developmental disabilities should be maximized and encouraged. Training may initially have to be done by individuals in the United States or other regions of Canada in which work with child victims with intellectual impairments is more common. There is some danger in training being done by an individual who has seen only a handful of clients in this population, as they seem more likely to generalize incorrectly from the experience of those individuals. All intake forms should be revised to include the documentation of any disability which the child has. This is an imperfect measure as has been discussed previously, however, no judgements can be made about the number of children being served, or the effectiveness of the agency in serving them unless this information is available.

b. **"Perceived" Accessibility**

The second step in making services accessible is for these services and agencies to do outreach to people with intellectual impairments. This step has only recently been started with regard to physical disabilities, for example, hearing impaired individuals are now told on some brochures that sign interpreters are available. This kind of outreach is necessary if those individuals with developmental disabilities are to know that the services are available to them.

c. **Agencies for those with intellectual impairments**

Those agencies whose mandate is provision of services to people with intellectual impairments must accept that the risk of sexual abuse is real. This acceptance is necessary to ensure that agencies will act appropriately in cases of allegations of sexual abuse. Education of these agencies in these terms is critical to the provision of services.

3. RESEARCH

a. **Prevalence of sexual abuse among children with intellectual impairments**

Documentation exists that sexual abuse is a problem for children with developmental disabilities. Research which is attempted should now be of a higher quality and more rigorous nature than that which has been done before. Hard's (1986) study is the best model available for the type of research which will yield the most information. An emphasis needs to be placed on the collection of information from individuals not previous sampled, for example those children and adolescents who are confined to institutions, and those children with limited verbal skills. Researchers must be creative both in their methods and approaches to the issue. In order for a complete picture to be obtained of the victimization which children experience, institutions must be opened up to research. Musick (05/87) has suggested that access to one institution's medical records would put an entirely different perspective on the abuse of children with developmental disabilities.

b. **Needs assessment**

It is clear that child victims of sexual abuse who happen to have an intellectual impairment are not being served adequately by the current system. Needs assessments for treatment programs, counselling services, and health care would be helpful. It is important to identify where victims are currently going for help, and where they are not. The need for this type of research should not delay the changes which are needed so urgently however.

c. **Sex offenders with intellectual impairments**

Research is needed to ascertain the number of sex offenders with a developmental disability in Canada. But more importantly, research is needed to establish the role of the disability in the commission of the offense (e.g., lack of sex education), the arrest of the offender (e.g., lacking the skills to keep the secret), or their treatment following arrest. Needs assessments have recently been carried out in Toronto with respect to the adolescent sex offender. This type of research is required across Canada for both adult and adolescent offenders.

d. **Treatment**

Research is needed desperately to establish the effectiveness of different treatment programs and counselling techniques to assist the child victim with an intellectual impairment. Research is also needed to investigate the range of signs and symptoms and types of disclosure exhibited by children with developmental disabilities. Research investigating the effectiveness of treatment programs and various techniques in the treatment of sex offenders with developmental disabilities is also required.

4. LEGAL REMEDIES

Bill C-15 passed the third and final reading in the summer of 1987 and was proclaimed in January 1988. It is hoped that the section of the Evidence Act which guarantees an interpreter for those parties or witnesses who speak a language other than that in which a trial is conducted, would be applied in the broadest manner possible to include the use of an interpreter for those individuals with limited but recognizable (to a known individual) verbal skills. These changes give the child and adolescent victims of sexual abuse who have an intellectual impairment access to the legal system comparable to the access experienced by other children and adolescents. It is crucial that these changes not be left to stand on their own. Rather they must be accompanied by the education of Crown attorneys and judges regarding the research on children's competency as witnesses as well as the information available on the ability of individuals with intellectual impairments to testify.

References

Aguilar, S. (1984). *Prosecuting Cases of Physical and Sexual Assault of the Mentally Retarded,* Prosecutors Notebook Volume III, California District Attorneys Association.

Alexander, J. (1979). Child abuse and the developmentally disabled: An overview. In *Child Abuse and Developmental Disabilities: Essays.* U.S. Department of Health Education and Welfare.

Allen, C. V. (1980). *Daddy's Girl.* New York: Wyndham.

Appelbaum, A.S. (1980). Developmental retardation in infants as a concomitant of physical child abuse. In G. Williams and J. Money (Eds.), *Traumatic Abuse and Neglect of Children at Home,* (pp. 304-310). Baltimore: John Hopkins University Press.

Armstrong, L. (1978). *Kiss Daddy Goodnight.* New York: Hawthorn Press.

A.W. 637 P. 2d 366 (Colo. 1981).

Badgley et al. (1984). *Committee on Sexual Offences Against Children and Youths.* Minister of Supply and Services Canada.

Bagley, C. & Ramsay, R. (1986). Sexual abuse in childhood: Psychosocial outcomes and implications for social work practice. *Journal of Social Work and Human Sexuality, 4,* 1-2, 33-47.

Bahrick, H.P., Bahrick, P.O. & Wittinger, R.P. (1975). Fifty years of memory for names and faces: A cross- sectional approach. *Journal of Experimental Psychology: General, 104,* 54-75.

Baladerian, N.J. (undated). *ICAN Child Sexual Abuse Task Force: Subcommittee report on developmentally disabled survivors.*

Baladerian, N.J. (1976). *How to Approach Sexuality.* Paper presented at the Southern California Regional American Association on Mental Deficiency Conference, Newport Beach, California, January 29.

Baladerian, N.J. (1985a). *Prevention of sexual exploitation of developmentally disabled adults.* Paper presented at the 1985 Convention of the California Association of Post-secondary Educators of the Disabled, Sacramento, California.

Baladerian, N.J. (1985b). *Response to: "Prosecuting cases of physical and sexual assault of the mentally retarded" issued by the California District Attorney's Association.*

Baladerian, N.J. with Dankowski, K. & Jackson, T. (1986). *Survivor, Volumes I, II, and III.* California Community Foundation.

Barth, R. & Blythe, B. (1983). The contribution of stress to child abuse. *Social Service Review,* September, 477-488.

Bender, L. & Blau, A. (1937). The reaction of children to sexual relations with adults. *American Journal of Orthopsychiatry, 7,* 500.

Bennett, B., Vockell, E., & Vockell, K. (1972). Sex education for EMR adolescent girls: An evaluation and some suggestions. *Journal for Special Educators of Mentally Retarded, 9,* 3-7.

Bernstein, N.R. (1985). Sexuality in mentally retarded adolescents. *Medical Aspects of Human Sexuality, 19*(11), 50-52, 57, 60-61.

Blomberg, P.S. (undated). *The Sexually Assaulted, Developmentally Delayed Person . . . The victim no one believes . . .* Fact sheet on informed consent assessment and evaluation procedures for persons with a developmental disability.

Blomberg, P.S. (1986). *Vulnerability issues of children with developmental disabilities: Sexual exploitation, the problems, solutions, and assessments.* Paper presented at Current Issues for Child Abuse Professionals conference, December 3.

Blomberg, P.S. (1987). *The Evaluation of a Prevention of Sexual Abuse Program for Persons with Developmental Disabilities.* Unpublished Master's Thesis. University of California at Davis.

Blumberg, M.L. (1979). Character disorders in traumatized and handicapped children. *American Journal of Psychotherapy, 33*(2), 201-213.

Brown, B.S. & Courtless, T.F. (1969). The mentally retarded offender. In R.C. Allen (Ed.), *Readings in Law and Psychiatry*, Baltimore: Johns Hopkins University Press.

Browne, A. & Finkelhor, D. (1986). Impact of child sexual abuse: A review of the research. *Psychological Bulletin, 99*(1), 66-77.

Burgess, A.W., Groth, A.N., Holmstrom, L.L. & Sgroi, S.M. (1978). *Sexual Assault of Children and Adolescents.* Lexington, MA: Lexington Books.

Burgess, A.W. & Holmstrom, L.L. (1978). Complicating factors in the sexual assault of adolescent victims. In A.W. Burgess et al., (Eds.) *Sexual Assault of Children and Adolescents.* Lexington, MA: Lexington Books.

Butler, S. (1978). *Conspiracy of Silence.* San Francisco, CA: New Glide.

Caffey, J. (1974). The whiplash shaken infant syndrome: Manual shaking by the extremities with whiplash-induced intracranial and intraocular bleedings, linked with residual permanent brain damage and mental retardation. *Pediatrics, 282*, 933-939.

Camblin, L.D. (1982). A survey of state efforts in gathering information on child abuse and neglect in handicapped populations. *Child Abuse and Neglect, 6*, 465-472.

Canadian Association for Community Living (CACL) (1986). *Brief to the Legislative Committee of the House of Commons on Bill C-15*, December 19.

Chamberlain, A., Rauh, J., Passer, A., McGrath, M., & Burket, R. (1984). Issues in fertility control for mentally retarded female adolescents: I. Sexual activity, sexual abuse, and contraception. *Pediatrics, 73*(4), 445-450.

Chi, M.T.H. (1978). Knowledge structures and memory development. In R. Siegler (Ed.), *Children's Thinking: What Develops?*; Hillsdale, NJ: Erlbaum.

Colby, I. & Colby, D. (1987). Videotaping the child sexual abuse victim. *Social Casework: The Journal of Contemporary Social Work*, February, 117-121.

Cole, S.S. (1986). Facing the challenges of sexual abuse in persons with disabilities. *Sexuality and Disability, 7*(3-4), 71-87.

Coleman, E.M. & Murphy, W.D. (1980). A survey of sexual attitudes and sex education programs among facilities for mentally retarded. *Applied Research in Mental Retardation, 1*(3-4), 269-276.

Committee on abuse of persons with disabilities. (1985).
Subcommittee of ICAN Task Force on Sexual Abuse Report.
*Results of Country-wide Regional Centres Survey on Abuse Reporting,
Follow-up, Professional Training.* August.

Conte, J.R. (1986). *A Look at Child Sexual Abuse.* National Committee
for Prevention of Child Abuse.

Conte, J.R. & Berliner, L. (1981). Sexual abuse of children:
Implications for practice. *Social Casework, 62*, 601-606.

Cowardin, N.W. (1986). *Preventing Sexual Exploitation of Adolescents with
Exceptional Needs.* Unpublished manuscript.

Cowardin, N.W. (1987). *Child Abuse and the Developmentally Disabled.*
Almansor Education Centre, January 16. Unpublished
manuscript.

Dawson, R. (1984). *The Abuse of Children in Foster Care: A study of
incidence, characteristics, and precipitating characters.* Toronto: Ontario
Association of Children's Aid Societies.

Dent, H.R. & Stephenson, G.M. (1979). Identification evidence:
Experimental investigations of factors affecting the reliability
of juvenile and adult witnesses. In D. P. Farrington, K.
Hawkins, & S.M. Lloyd-Bostock (Eds.), *Psychology, Law, and Legal
Processes;* Atlantic Highlands, NJ: Humanities Press.

de Young, M. (1986). A conceptual model for judging the
truthfulness of a young child's allegation of sexual abuse.
American Journal of Orthopsychiatry, 56(4), 550-559.

Diamond, L. & Judes, P. (1983). Child abuse in cerebral palsied
population. *Developmental Medicine and Child Neurology, 26,*
169-174.

Dillon, J. (1980). *Medical Treatment and Criminal Law,* Law Reform
Commission of Canada, Working Paper 26.

Durkin, R. (1982). No one will thank you: First thoughts on
reporting institutional abuse. In R. Hanson (Ed.) *Institutional
Abuse of Children and Youth.* Child and Youth Services, 4(1-2),
109-114.

Edgerton, R.B. & Dingman, H.F. (1964). Good reasons for bad
supervision: "Dating" in a hospital for the mentally retarded.
The Psychiatric Quarterly Supplement, Part 2, 1-13.

Edmonson, B., McCombs, K. & Wish, J. (1979). What retarded
adults believe about sex. *American Journal of Mental Deficiency, 84,*
11-18.

Edmonson, B. & Wish, J. (1975). Sex knowledge and attitudes of
moderately retarded males. *American Journal of Mental Deficiency,
80,* 172-179.

Elierstein, N.S. & Canavan, W. (1980). Sexual abuse of boys. *American Journal of the Diseases of Childhood, 134*, 255-257.

Elmer, E. & Gregg, G.S. (1967). Developmental characteristics of abused children. *Pediatrics, 40,* 596-602.

Elonen, A.S. & Zwarensteyn, S.B. (1975). Sexual trauma in young blind children. *New Outlook for the Blind, 69,* 440-442.

Endicott, O. (1987). To tell the truth: Can our courts hear the evidence of persons with a mental disability? *Entourage, 2*(2), 23-25.

Fifield, B.B. (1986). Ethical issues related to sexual abuse of disabled persons. *Sexuality and Disability, 7*(3-4), 102-109.

Finkelhor, D. (1979). *Sexually Victimized Children.* New York: Free Press.

Finkelhor, D. (1984). *Child Sexual Abuse: New theory and research.* New York: Free Press.

Finkelhor, D. & Araji, S. (1983). The prevention of child sexual abuse: A review of current approaches. *SAPR,* df*17,* 21 Dec.

Finkelhor, D. & Browne, A. (1985). The traumatic impact of child sexual abuse: a conceptualization. *American Journal of Orthopsychiatry, 5*5(4), 530-541.

Finkelhor, D. & Associates (1986). *A Sourcebook on Child Sexual Abuse.* Beverly Hills, CA: Sage Publications.

Fischer, H.L. & Krajicek, M. (1974). Sexual development of the moderately retarded child: Level of information and parental attitudes. *Mental Retardation, 12*(3), 28-30.

Fisher, G. & Field, S. (1985). Self-protection education for disabled youth: A priority need. *CDEI Journal, 8,* 7-16.

Forchuk, C., Pitkeathly, Cook, Allen & St. Denis McDonald (1984). Sex education and the mentally retarded. *Canadian Nurse, 80* (April), 36-39.

Forseth, L.B. & Brown, A. (1981). A survey of intrafamilial sexual abuse treatment centres: Implications for intervention. *Child Abuse and Neglect, 5,* 177-186.

Foxx, R.M. (1976). The use of overcorrection to eliminate the public disrobing (stripping) of retarded women. *Behavior Research and Therapy, 14,* 53-60.

Friedman, E. (1972). Missing in the life of the retarded individual: Reflections on Sol Gordon's paper. *Journal of Special Education, 5,* 365.

Friedman, P.R. (1976). *The Rights of Mentally Retarded Persons.* New York: Avon Books.

Friedrich, W.N. & Boriskin, J.A. (1978). Primary prevention of child abuse: Focus on the special child. *Hospital and Community Psychiatry, 29*(4), 248-251.

Friedrich, W.N. & Reams, R.A. (in press). Course of psychological symptoms in sexually abused young children. *Psychotherapy.*

Gager, N. & Scheier, C. (1976). *Sexual Assault: Confronting rape in America.* New York: Grossett and Dunlop.

Gebhard, P.H., Gagnon, J.H., Pomeroy, W.B. & Christianson, C.V. (1965). *Sex Offenders: An analysis of types.* New York: Harper & Row.

Geist, C.S., Knudson, C. & Sorenson, K. (1979). Practical sex education for the mentally retarded. *Journal of Applied Rehabilitation Counseling, 10*(4), 186-189.

Gil, D.G. (1970). Violence against children. *Journal of Marriage and the Family, 33,* 637-648.

Gil, E. (1979). *Handbook for understanding and preventing abuse and neglect of children in out-of-home care.* San Francisco Child Abuse Council.

Gil, E. (1982a). *Foster Parenting Abused Children.* National Committee for Prevention of Child Abuse.

Gil, E. (1982b). Institutional abuse of children in out-of- home care. In R. Hanson (Ed.), *Institutional Abuse of Children and Youth.* New York: The Haworth Press, 4(1-2), 7-13.

Glaser, D. & Bentovim, A. (1979). Abuse and risk to handicapped and chronically ill children. *Child Abuse and Neglect, 3,* 565-575.

Goodman, G.S. & Helgeson, V.S. (1985). *Child Sexual Assault: Children's memory and the law.* Papers from a National Policy Conference on Legal Reforms in Child Sexual Abuse Cases, National Legal Resource Center for Child Advocacy and Protection, Washington, DC, March, 43-60.

Goodman, G.S., Hirschman, J. & Rudy, L. (1987). *Children's Testimony: Research and Policy Implications.* Paper presented at Society for Research in Child Development meetings, Baltimore, MD, April.

Goodman, L. (1973). The sexual rights of the retarded — A dilemma for parents. *The Family Coordinator, 22,* 472-474.

Goodwin, J. (1981). Suicide attempts in sexual abuse victims and their mothers. *Child Abuse and Neglect, 5,* 217-221.

Green, F.C. (1976). What will it cost the child if I don't report? In M.A. Thomas (Ed.), *Children Alone: What can be done about abuse and neglect.* The Council for Exceptional Children.

Green, D.T. (1983). A human sexuality program for developmentally disabled women in a sheltered workshop setting. *Sexuality and Disability, 6*(1), 20-24.

Greenland, C. (1983). Sex law reform in an international perspective: England and Wales and Canada. *Bulletin of the American Academy of Psychiatry and the Law, 11*(4), 309-330.

Hall, J. (1974). Sexual behavior. In J. Wortis (Ed.), *Mental Retardation and Developmental Disabilities — An Annual Review, Vol. VI.* New York: Brunner/Mazel, 178-212.

Hall, J.E. & Morris, H.L. (1976). Sexual knowledge and attitudes of institutionalized and non-institutionalized retarded adolescents. *American Journal of Mental Deficiency, 80,* 382-387.

Hall, J.E., Morris, H.L. & Barker, H.R. (1973). Sexual knowledge and attitudes of mentally retarded adolescents. *American Journal of Mental Deficiency, 77,* 706-709.

Hard, S. (1986). *Sexual Abuse of the Developmentally Disabled: A case study.* Paper presented at the National Conference of Executives of Associations for Retarded Citizens, Omaha, Nebraska, Oct. 22.

Herman, J.L. (1981). *Father-Daughter Incest.* Cambridge, MA: Harvard University Press.

Hirayama, H. (1979). Management of the sexuality of the mentally retarded in institutions: Problems and issues. In D. Kunkel (Ed.), *Sexual Issues in Social Work.* Honolulu, Hawaii: University of Hawaii, School of Social Work.

Hunter, R.S., Kilstrom, & Loda (1985). Sexually abused children: Identifying masked presentations in a medical setting. *Child Abuse and Neglect, 9*(1), 17-25.

Jenny, C., Sutherland, S.E. & Sandahl, B.B. (1986). Developmental approach to preventing the sexual abuse of children. *Pediatrics, 78*(6), 1034-1038.

Johnson, M.K. & Foley, M.A. (1984). Differentiating fact from fantasy: The reliability of children's memory. *Journal of Social Issues, 40*(2), 33-50.

Johnson, W.R. & Kempton, W. (1981). *Sex education and counseling of special groups: The mentally and physically disabled, ill and elderly.* Springfield, IL: Charles C. Thomas Publisher.

Jones, D.P.H. & McQuiston, M. (1984). Interviewing the sexually abused child — II Principles and Practice. In D.C. Bross (Ed.), *Multidisciplinary Advocacy for Mistreated Children.* Denver, CO: National Association of Council for Children.

Katan, A. (1973). Children who were raped. *Psychoanalytic Study of the Child, 28*, 208-224.

Kempe, C.H. (1985). Introduction: International perspectives and prospects regarding assault against children. In J. H. Meier (Ed.), *Assault Against Children: Why it happens, How to stop it*. San Diego, CA: College-Hill Press.

Kempton, W. (1977). The mentally retarded person. In H.L. Gochros & J.S. Gochros (Eds.), *The Sexually Oppressed*. New York: Association Press.

Kercher & McShane, M. (1984). The prevalence of child sexual abuse victimization in an adult sample of Texas residents. *Child Abuse and Neglect, 8*, 495-502.

Kline, D.F. (1979). The consequences of neglected cases. In A.M. Thomas (Ed.), *Children Alone: What can be done about abuse and neglect* (pp. 53-60). Reston, VA: Council for Exceptional Children.

Knopp, F.H. (1984). *Retraining Adult Sex Offenders: Methods and models*. Syracuse, NY: Safer Society Press.

Langevin, R. (1983). *Sexual Strands: Understanding and treating sexual anomalies in men*. Hillsdale, NJ: Erlbaum.

Lewis, M. & Sarrell, P.M. (1969). Some psychological aspects of seduction, incest and rape in childhood. *Journal of the American Academy of Child Psychiatry, 8*.

Loftus, E.F. (1979). *Eyewitness Testimony*. Cambridge, MA: Harvard University Press.

Longo, R.E. & Gochenour, C. (1981). Sexual assault of handicapped individuals. *Journal of Rehabilitation, 47*, 24-27.

MacDonald, J.M. (1973). *Indecent Exposure*. Springfield, IL: Charles C. Thomas.

MacPherson, C. (1984, February 6). Metro defence courses teach disabled to survive. *Toronto Star*, B3.

Markin, K. (1987, January 29). Jail decision boosts rights for prisoners. *Globe and Mail*.

Marin, B.V., Homes, D.L., Guth, M. & Kovac, P. (1979). The potential of children as eyewitnesses. *Law and Human Behavior, 3*(4), 295-306.

Marquis, K.H., Marshall, J. & Oskamp, S. (1972). Testimony validity as a function of question form, atmosphere, and item difficulty. *Journal of Applied Social Psychology, 2*, 167-186.

Marshall, W.L., Barbaree, H.E. & Christophe, D. (1986). Sexual offenders against female children: Sexual preference for age of victims and type of behavior. *Canadian Journal of Behavioral Science, 18*(4), 424-439.

Martin, H.P., Beezley, P., Conway, E.F., & Kempe, C.H. (1974). The development of abused children. *Advances in Pediatrics, 21,* 25-73.

Mathews, F. (undated). *Adolescent Sex Offenders: A Needs Study.* Central Toronto Youth Services.

Mayer, A. (1983). *Incest: A treatment manual for therapy with victims, spouses and offenders.* Holmes Beach, FL: Learning Publications.

McCauley, J., Gorman, R.L. & Guzinski, G. (1986). Toluidine blue in the detection of perineal lacerations in pediatric and adolescent sexual abuse victims. *Pediatrics, 78*(6), 1039-1043.

McKague, C. (1981). The competency of a mentally handicapped person to testify. *Just Cause,* 19-22.

Mian, M., Wehrspann, W., Klajner-Diamond, H., LeBaron, D. & Winder, C. (1986). Review of 125 children 6 years of age and under who were sexually abused. *Child Abuse and Neglect, 10,* 223-229.

Miller, P. (1976). Blaming the victim of child molestation: An empirical analysis. (Doctoral dissertation, Northwestern University). Dissertation Abstracts International. (University microfilms No. 77-10069).

Ministry of Community and Social Services (1978). *Guidelines for the Investigation of Resident Abuse and Suspected Resident Abuse in Facilities for the Mentally Retarded.*

Minnesota Program for Victims of Sexual Assault (1983). *Are Children with Disabilities Vulnerable to Sexual Abuse?*

Mitchell, L.K. (1985). *Behavioral Intervention in the Sexual Problems of Mentally Handicapped Individuals: In residential and home settings.* Springfield, IL: Charles C. Thomas Publisher.

In the interest of MKR — a child, 515 Southwestern Reporter 2d 467 (Mo. 1974).

Moglia, R. (1986). Sexual abuse and disability. *SIECUS Report,* March, 9-10.

Mohr, J.W., Turner, R.W. & Jerry, M.B. (1964). *Pedophilia and Exhibitionism.* Toronto: University of Toronto Press.

Morgenstern, M. (1973). Community attitudes toward sexuality of the retarded. In F.F. de la Cruz & G.D. LaVeck (Eds.), *Human Sexuality and the Mentally Retarded.* New York: Brunner/Mazel.

Morse, C., Sahler, O. & Friedman, S. (1970). A three-year follow-up study of abused and neglected children. *American Journal of Diseases of Children, 120,* 439-446.

Mrazek, P.B. & Kempe, C.H. (Eds.) (1981). *Sexually Abused Children and Their Families.* New York: Pergamon Press.

Murphy, W.D., Coleman, E.M. & Abel, G.G. (1983). Human sexuality in the mentally retarded. In J. Matson & F. Andrasik (Eds.), *Treatment Issues and Innovations in Mental Retardation.* New York: Plenum Press.

Murphy, W.D., Coleman, E.M. & Haynes, (1983). Treatment and evaluation issues with the mentally retarded sex offender. In J.G. Greer & I.R. Stuart (Eds.), *The Sexual Aggressor.* New York: Van Nostrand Reinhold.

Murphy, L. & Della Corte, S. (1987). Abuse and the special child. *Special Parent Special Child, 3*(1), 1-6.

Musick, J.L. (1984). Patterns of institutional sex assault. *Response to Violence in the Family and Sexual Assault, 7*(3), 1-2, 10-11.

PACER (1986). Parent Advocacy Coalition for Educational Rights, *A Resource Manual on Child Abuse.* Minneapolis.

Per-lee, M.S. (1981). *Victim Witness Project for the Handicapped: Victim justice for disabled Persons: A resource manual.* Washington, DC: Gallaudet College.

Perrin, J.C., et al. (1976). A considered approach to sterilization of mentally retarded youth. *American Journal of Diseases of Children, 130,* 288-290.

Peters, S.D. (1984). The relationship between childhood sexual victimization and adult depression among Afro-American and white women. Unpublished doctoral dissertation. University of California at Los Angeles. (University Microfilms, No. 84-28, 555).

Poirier, P. (1986, November 28). Testing of child witnesses assailed as abuse incentive. *The Globe and Mail.*

Price, J.M. & Valdiserri, E.V. (1981). Childhood sexual abuse: A recent review of the literature. *Journal of American Medical Women Association, 36,* 232-234.

Rimsza, M.E. & Niggemann, E.H. (1982). Medical evaluation of sexually abused children: A review of 311 cases. *Pediatrics, 69,* 8-14.

Rioux, M.H. (1979). *Sterilization: Implications for mentally retarded and mentally ill persons.* Working Paper 24. Law Reform Commission of Canada.

Rogers, K. (1972). For her own good. *Law and Society Review, 7*(2), 223-246.

Rose, L. (1986). Sexual assault in special needs populations. *SIECUS Report, 1*(1), 20-26.

Rush, F. (1980). *The Best Kept Secret: Sexual abuse of children*. New York: McGraw-Hill.

Rush, F. (1983). *The Freudian Cover-up*. Article distributed at Counselling the Sexual Abuse Survivor Conference in Winnipeg, 1985.

Russell, D.E.H. (1983). The incidence and prevalence of intrafamilial and extrafamilial sexual abuse of female children. *Child Abuse and Neglect: The International Journal, 7*, 2.

Russell, D.E.H. (1984). *Sexual Exploitation: Rape, child sexual abuse, and workplace harassment*. California: Sage Publications, Inc.

Russell, D.E.H. (1986). The incest legacy: Why today's abused children become tomorrow's victims of rape. *The Sciences*, March/April, 28-32.

Ryerson, E. (1984). Sexual abuse and self-protection education for developmentally disabled youth: A priority need. *SIECUS Report, 13*(1), 6-7.

Sanders, G.S. & Warnick, D. (1981). Some conditions maximizing eyewitness accuracy: A learning/memory model. *Journal of Criminal Justice, 9*, 136-142.

Sandgrund, A., Gaines, R.W. & Green, A.H. (1974). Child abuse and mental retardation: A problem of cause and effect. *American Journal of Mental Deficiency, 79*(3), 327-330.

Sank, C. & LaFleche, E. (1981). Special sisters: Health issues for mentally retarded women. *Off Our Backs*, May, p. 26.

Santamour, M.B. & West, B. (1978). The retarded offender and corrections. *Mental Retardation and the Law*, October, 25-37.

Schilling, R.F., Kirkham, & Schinke, (1986). Do child protection services neglect developmentally disabled children? *Education and Training of the Mentally Retarded*, March, 21-26.

Seagull, E.A.W. & Scheurer, S.L. (1986). Neglected and abused children of mentally retarded parents. *Child Abuse and Neglect, 10*, 493-500.

Selling, L.S. (1939). Types of behavior manifested by feeble-minded sex offenders. *Proceedings from the American Association on Mental Deficiency, 44*, 178-186.

Sengstock, W.L. & Vergason, G.A. (1970). Issues in sex education for the retarded. *Education and Training of the Mentally Retarded, 5*, 99-103.

Sgroi, S.M. (1982). *Handbook of Clinical Intervention in Child Sexual Abuse*. Lexington, MA: Lexington Books.

Shore, D.A. (1982). Sexual abuse and sexual education in child-caring institutions. *Journal of Social Work and Human Sexuality,* 1(Fall-Winter), 171-184.

Silber, T.J. & Controni, M.S. (1982). Clinical spectrum of pharyngeal gonorrhea in children and adolescents: Report of 16 patients. *Journal of Adolescent Health Care,* 1 July.

Silbert, M.H. & Pines, A.M. (1981). Sexual child abuse as an antecedent to prostitution. *Child Abuse and Neglect,* 5, 407-411.

Simonds, J.F. (1980). Sexual behaviors in retarded children and adolescents. *Journal of Developmental and Behavioral Pediatrics,* 1(4), 173-179.

Singer, D. & Reveson, T. (1978). *How a Child Thinks.* New York: New American Library.

Solomons, G. (1979). Child abuse and developmental disabilities. *Developmental Medical Child Neurology, 21,* 101-106.

Souther, M.D. (undated). *Developmentally disabled, abused and neglected children: A high risk/high need population.* Photocopy.

Starr, R.H., Dietrich, K.N., Fischoff, J., Ceresnie, S. & Zweier, D. (1984). The contribution of handicapping conditions to child abuse. *Topics in Early Childhood Special Education,* 4(1), 55-69.

Stevens, D. & Berliner, L. (1979). Special techniques for child witnesses. In L.G. Schultz (Ed.), *The Sexual Victimology of Youth,* Springfield, IL: Charles C. Thomas.

Stokes, R.E. (1964). A research approach to sexual offenses involving children. *Canadian Journal of Corrections,* 6, 87-94.

Summit, R. (1983). Recognition and treatment of child sexual abuse. In C. Hollingsworth (Ed.), *Providing for the Emotional Health of the Pediatric Patient.* New York: Spectrum Publishers.

Summit, R. & Kryso, J. (1978). Sexual abuse of children: A clinical spectrum. *American Journal of Orthopsychiatry,* 48(2), 237-251.

Szymanski, L.S. (1977). Psychiatric diagnostic evaluation of mentally retarded individuals. *Journal of the American Academy of Child Psychiatry, 16,* 67-87.

Szymanski, L.S. & Jansen, P.E. (1980). Assessment of sexuality and sexual vulnerability of retarded persons. In L.S. Szymanski & P. Tanguey (Eds.), *Emotional Disorders of Mentally Retarded Persons.* Baltimore: University Park Press.

Turnbull, H. (Ed.) (1977). *Consent Handbook.* Washington, DC: American Association on Mental Deficiency, Special Publication #3.

Varley, C.K. (1984). Schizophreniform psychoses in mentally retarded adolescent girls following sexual assault. *American Journal of Psychiatry,* 141(4), 593-594.

Vigilanti, M.A. (undated). *Sexual abuse and developmentally disabled women and children: A current perspective.* Photocopy.

Virkkunen, M. (1974). Incest offences and alcoholism. *Medicine Science and the Law.,* 14, 124.

Watson, J.D. (1984). Talking about the Best Kept Secret: Sexual abuse and children with disabilities. *The Exceptional Parent,* September, 15-22.

Whitcomb, D. (1982). *Assisting Child Victims of Sexual Abuse (for Special Needs Victims).* Frederick, MD: Aspen Publishers Inc.

Whitman, W.P. & Quinsey, V.L. (1981). Heterosocial skill training for institutionalized rapists and child molesters. *Canadian Journal of Behavioral Science,* 13(2), 105-114.

Women Against Rape (WAR) (undated). *Myths about the Sexual Assault of Persons Labeled Mentally Retarded/Developmentally Disabled/Chronically Mentally Ill.* Assault Prevention Training Project, Columbus, Ohio.

Wooden, K. (1976). *Weeping in the Playtime of Others: America's Incarcerated Children.* New York: McGraw- Hill Book Company.

Worthington, G.M. (1984). Sexual exploitation and abuse of people with disabilities. *Response,* 7(2), March/April, 7-8.

Wyatt, G.E. (1985). The sexual abuse of Afro-American and white American women in childhood. *Child Abuse and Neglect,* 9, 507-519.

CONSULTATIONS

15/05/87	Anderson Kent, Cordelia: Educator, Sexual Abuse Prevention Illusion Theatre, Minneapolis, Minnesota
06/87	Workshop: Prevention
28/05/87	Antell, Steve: Adult Protective Services, Social and Rehabilitation Services, Vermont.
28/05/87	Authier, Karen: Administrative Director, Center for Abused Handicapped Children at Boystown, Omaha, Nebraska
06/87	Barbaree, Howard: Kingston Sexual Offenders Clinic, Department of Psychiatry, Queen's University, Kingston, Ontario
06/87	Barrett, Mike: SIECAN (Sex Information and Education Council of Canada) Toronto, Ontario
02/85	Berliner, Lucy: Therapist, Seattle, Washington Workshop: Young child victims, Presented at the Winnipeg Conference, Counselling the Sexual Abuse Survivor.
25/05/87	Birrell, Joan: Barbara Shleiffer Clinic, Toronto, Ontario
06/87	Blomberg, Patti: Association for Retarded Citizens & Doctoral Candidate at University of California at Davis

15/05/87   Brand, Judith: Ministry of Education, Special Education Division, British Columbia.

06/87   Croezen, Robert: Workshop: Interviewing, Child Abuse Coordinator, Kitchener, Ontario

22/05/87   Daro, Debra: National Commission for the Prevention of Child Abuse (NCPCA), Chicago, Illinois.

05/87   Davies, Joan: Joan Davies Associates, Family Life Educator, Middletown, New Jersey

06/87   Dawson, Ross: Workshop: Institutional Abuse, Executive Director, Family and Child Services, Woodstock, Ontario.

13/07/87   Dickey, Jo: The Community Living Society, Vancouver, British Columbia

19/05/87   Doucette, Joanne: Disabled Women's Network, (DAWN) Toronto, Ontario

05/88   Duffet, Pauline: Counsellor, Peterborough Rape Crisis Centre, Ontario

16/07/87   Eakin, Lynn: J.D. Griffin Adolescent Centre, Toronto, Ontario

29/06/87   Endicott, Orville: Canadian Association for Community Living, Toronto, Ontario

04/87   Finkler, Lilith: Toronto, Ontario

06/87   Garfinkel, Lily: Coordinator, PACER (Parent Advocacy Coalition for Educational Rights), Minnesota

25/05/87   Gould, Gayle: Metropolitan Toronto Special Committee on Child Abuse

03/06/87   Griffiths, Dorothy: York Behavioral Management Program, York Central Hospital, Toronto, Ontario.

06/87   Hallet, Shelley: Assistant Crown Attorney, Toronto, Ontario, Workshop: New Laws, New Possibilities.

11/06/87   Hansen, Susan: Program Supervisor, Association for Retarded Citizens, Denver, Colorado.

22/05/87   Hard, Suzanne (with research from William Plumb): Researcher, San Diego, California

01/06/87   Heusen, Ann: Rehabilitation Studies, University of Calgary, Alberta

25/05/87   Holmes, Carole: Program Supervisor, COMSOC — Ontario Ministry of Community and Social Services

17/07/87   Hyman, Batya: Therapist, Jamaica Plain, Massachusetts

01/06/87   Knopp, Faye Honey: Therapist/Author, Syracuse, New York

05/87   Krents, Elisabeth: Project Director, The Lexington Centre Child Abuse and Disabled Children Project, Jackson Heights, New York.

06/87   Lefkowitz, Myra: Workshop: Child Witnesses, Community Liaison, Metro Special Committee on Child Abuse, Toronto

20/05/87   Loney, Grace: Canadian Legal Advocacy Information and Research Association of the Disabled (CLAIR), Ottawa, Ontario

15/05/87   Lyster, Kim: Project Coordinator, Rights Now Project, British Columbians for Mentally Handicapped People

22/05/87   MacPherson, Cathy: PUSH Ontario

28/05/87   Marlett, Nancy: Director, Dinsdale Centre, Calgary, Alberta

20/05/87   Martin, Mariruth: Toronto Rape Crisis Center, Counsellor

15/05/87   Musick, Judith: Researcher, Institute for the Study of Sexual Assault, San Francisco, California

22/05/87   Nannarone, Dianne: Women's College Hospital Sexual Assault Unit, Toronto, Ontario.

15/07/87   Park, Peter: Self-advocacy specialist, People First, Toronto, Ontario

15/05/87   Purmort, Sheryl: Program Specialist, Minnesota Program for Victims of Sexual Assault, Dept. of Corrections

22/05/87   Reier, Suzanne: Researcher/Educator, Berkeley, California

16/07/87   Richler, Diane: Canadian Association for Community Living (CACL), Toronto, Ontario

21/05/87   Rodgers, Barbara: Program Manager, Thistletown Regional Centre, SAFE-T Program, Ontario

06/87   Russell, Diana: Researcher, Professor of Sociology Mills College, Oakland, California
Lecture: Research — Effective Utilization in Treatment and Prevention.

15/05/87   San Francisco Child Abuse Council

19/05/87   Seger, Linda: Office of Child Abuse Prevention,
           California
15/05/87   Shaman, Ellen: Seattle Rape Relief Developmental
           Disabilities Project
01/06/87   Simpson, Kathy: Educator, Planned Parenthood of
           Shasta-Diablo, California
20/05/87   Stiggall, Lynne: Educator
13/07/87   Udell, Rob: Maplehurst Correctional Centre, Milton,
           Ontario
15/07/87   Worrell, Bill: People First, Toronto, Ontario

Table 1.*

Abuse Reports Comparison

	State of California		King County, WA	
	Number	%	Number	%
Population (normal)	24,330,000	100	1,269,750	100
Population (DD)	2,919,600	12	152,370	12
Child abuse reports (total)	97,329	.004	unknown	—
Sexual abuse reports (total)	5,840	.00024	unknown	—
Sexual abuse reports (DD)	unknown	—	150	.00098

* From Cowardin (1987).

Figure 1.*
Four Preconditions of Child Sexual Abuse

I.   Predisposition to abuse experience
  1. male sex-role socialization
  2. childhood sexual abuse experience
  3. effects of exposure to pornography

II. Reduction of Internal Inhibitions
  1. minimization of harm done
  2. cultural view of female sexuality as commodity and children as property
  3. cultural supports for predatory male sexuality
  4. child not related by blood
  5. alcohol consumption
  6. pornography
  7. sexualization of children in the mass media

III. Reduction of Social Inhibitions
  1. pornography
  2. male dominance/structural power
  3. power disparity between adults and children

IV. Reduction of Child's Resistance
    Nine risk factors (see Figure 2)

* From Russell (06/87).

Figure 2.*
Finkelhor's Nine Risk Factors

1. Child is emotionally deprived
2. Child is socially isolated
3. Child knows adult
4. Child has special fondness for adult
5. Child is vulnerable to incentives offered by adult
6. Child feels helpless and powerless
7. Child is ignorant of what is happening
8. Child is sexually repressed and has sexual curiosity
9. Coercion

* From Russell (06/87).

Figure 3.
*Behavioral Indicators of Child Sexual Abuse**

1. Overly compliant behavior.
2. Acting-out, aggressive behavior.
3. Pseudomature behavior.
4. Hints about sexual activity.
5. Persistent and inappropriate sexual play with peers or toys or with themselves, or sexually aggressive behavior with others.
6. Detailed and age-inappropriate understanding of sexual behavior (especially by young children).
7. Arriving early at school and leaving late with few, if any, absences.
8. Poor peer relationships or inability to make friends.
9. Lack of trust, particularly with significant others.
10. Nonparticipation in school and social activities.
11. Inability to concentrate in school.
12. Sudden drop in school performance.
13. Extraordinary fear of males (in cases of male perpetrator and female victim).
14. Seductive behavior with males (in cases of male perpetrator and female victim).
15. Running away from home.
16. Sleep disturbances.
17. Regressive behavior.
18. Withdrawal.
19. Clinical depression.
20. Suicidal feelings.

* From Sgroi (1982, p. 40-41).
Copyright ©1982 (*Assault*), D.C. Heath Canada Limited.
Reprinted by permission.

Figure 4.

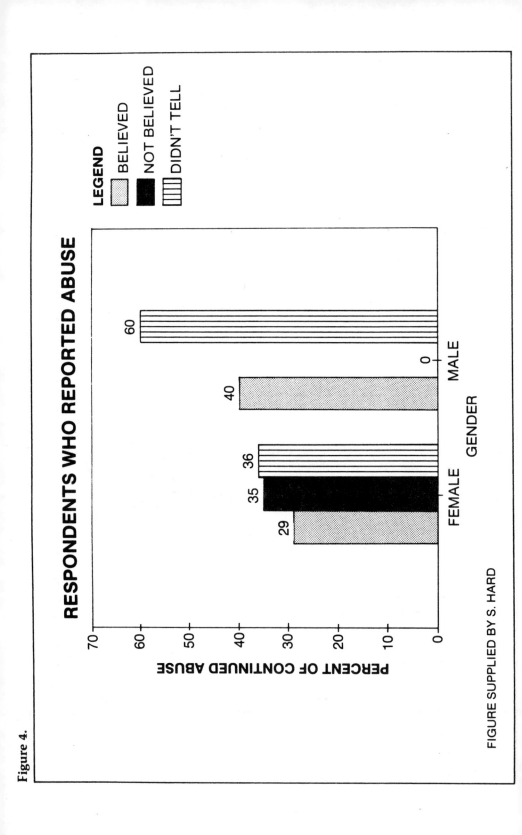

RESPONDENTS WHO REPORTED ABUSE

FIGURE SUPPLIED BY S. HARD

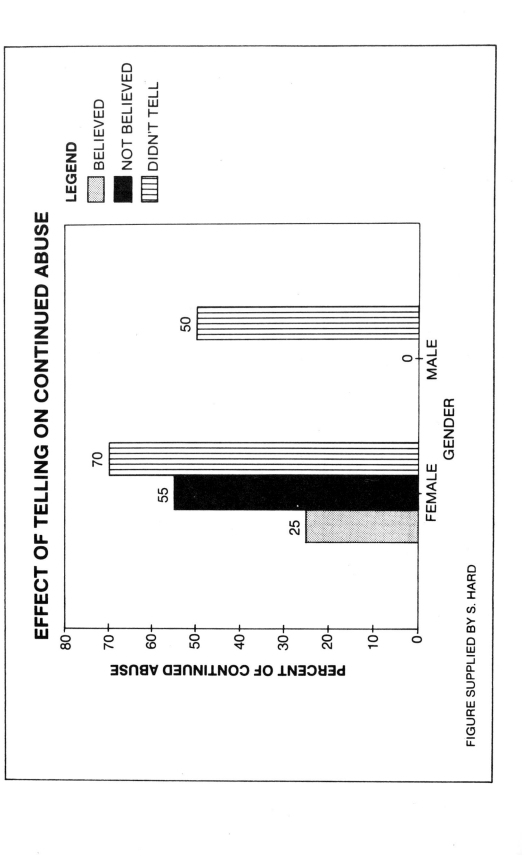

EFFECT OF TELLING ON CONTINUED ABUSE

LEGEND
BELIEVED
NOT BELIEVED
DIDN'T TELL

PERCENT OF CONTINUED ABUSE

GENDER

FEMALE

MALE

25

55

70

50

0

FIGURE SUPPLIED BY S. HARD

Figure 6.
*Initial Interview with Handicapped Victims**

1. Identify the handicap (e.g., comprehension level, physical speech, or hearing handicap; psychiatric or social problem).
2. Determine if the handicap will interfere with the interview and, if necessary, get help or advice from a family member or another staff person who has dealt with such clients.
3. Assess the impact of the rape on the victim's behavior (i.e., ask family members if this is a usual response to stress and/or what changes they have noted in the child's behavior).
4. Proceed with the usual protocol, adapting it to meet the stress level of the adolescent. Be prepared to take extra time with the victim and the family.
5. Be alert to avoid projecting stereotyped labels onto handicapped victims and, instead, carefully observe, assess, and talk with the victim and family in a respectful and kind manner, fully acknowledging the impact of the victimization.
6. Record the interview in language that respects the adolescent and the family but still objectively reports your findings.
7. Be prepared to work in a collaborative way with other staff already involved with the victim. Obtain permission from the victim first to talk with the agency, and then keep the victim informed, making sure the agency knows you are reporting back to the victim and family.

* From Burgess and Holmstrom (1987, p. 72-73.)
Copyright ©1978 (*Handbook*), D.C. Heath Canada Limited.

EFFECT OF SEX ED ON ABUSE

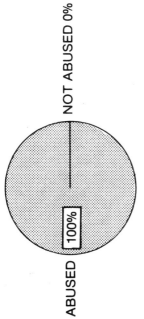

ABUSED 12%

NOT ABUSED 88%

FEMALES WITH SEX ED

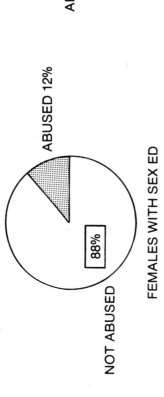

ABUSED 20%

NOT ABUSED 80%

MALES WITH SEX ED

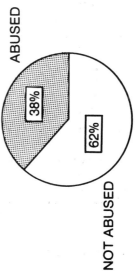

NOT ABUSED 0%

ABUSED 100%

FEMALES WITHOUT SEX ED

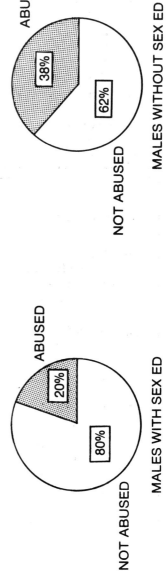

ABUSED 38%

NOT ABUSED 62%

MALES WITHOUT SEX ED

Figure 8.
*Rule Topics**

1. discipline
2. touching
3. talking
4. secrets
5. privacy
6. boundaries
7. sexual climate
8. clothing
9. alone or witness

* From a workshop on Institutional Abuse presented by
  Ross Dawson (06/87).

Figure 9.
*Avoiding Complaints**

A. Preparation
   - obtain full information re: child
   - training to deal with child's needs
   - plan of care

B. Follow Procedures
   - follow discipline policy
   - 'witness'
   - keep notes

C. Open Talk
   - keep social worker informed positive or negative
   - ask for help early
   - obtain support/relief when needed
   - assessment/medical help
   - training for foster mothers *and* fathers

* From a workshop on Institutional Abuse by Ross Dawson (06/87).

Figure 10.
*Cognitive Skills to be Assessed**

1. Recognition and recalling of faces may be an easy task, as no rehearsal is required.
2. Auditory memory problems may make it difficult to recall communication.
3. Recollection of several conversations, precise times and addresses may interfere with the person who has a developmental disability's ability to discuss the facts of the incidence [sic] with the interviewer.
4. Associated deficits in articulation, language processing and verbal skills may further jeopardize communication.
5. It is critical to assess the individual's cognitive strengths and weaknesses specifically on an individual basis in order to arrive at a just and meaningful competency determination.
6. Many individuals with a developmental delay may know that rape is wrong without having a clear idea of what rape means or what wrong means.
7. Oftentimes the interview will be to determine the individual's mental status at the time of the offense. This can create problems in view of the multiple cognitive defects of persons with retardation. It is critical to try to obtain a detailed description of the individuals activity on the day of the alleged offense, in addition to the detailed history of the offense itself. Additional information should be obtained from family members, any witnesses and police reports, in order to corroborate or refute the individuals own impressions.
8. Look for the individuals degree of passivity, and susceptibility to suggestion.

* From Blomberg (undated).

Figure 11
The Behavioral Assessment and Treatment of Sex Offenders.

	PROBLEM AREAS	TREATMENT METHODS	ASSESSMENT METHODS
Arousal variables	Excessive arousal to deviant stimuli	Aversion-suppression methods 1. Covert sensitization 2. Electrical aversion 3. Odor aversion 4. Chemical aversion 5. Biofeedback-assisted suppression 6. Satiation	Penile recordings Self-report Clinical interviews
	Deficit arousal to nondeviant sexual stimuli	General of arousal to nondeviant cues 1. Masturbatory conditioning 2. Exposure 3. Fading 4. Systematic desensitization	
Social skills deficits	Heterosocial skills Assertive skills	Heterosocial skills training Assertive training	Behavioral role-playing procedures Self-report inventories Clinical interviews
Sexual behavior	Sexual dysfunction Sexual knowledge	Therapy Sex education	Sexual inventories Sex education test Clinical interviews
Cognitive/social	Attitudes Perception Discrimination	?	Burt scale ?

APPENDIX A

Prevention Program	Target audience
Illusion Theatre (Anderson)	mild to moderate disability
Self-protection for the Handicapped (Fisher, 1982)	moderate disability
Special Education Curriculum on Sexual Exploitation (Seattle Rape Relief)	mild disability (ages 6 to adult)
No-Go-Tell	mild to severe disability (pre-school to adult)
What if . . . (Cowardin, 1986)	mild to moderate disability
Circles (Champagne & Walker-Hirsch, 1983)	mild to moderate disability
Preventing Sexual Abuse of Persons with Disabilities (O'Day, 1983)	mild to moderate disability
Assault Prevention Education (Women Against Rape, undated)	mild to moderate disability (adolescent to adult)

FOOTNOTES

1 The unethical nature of the solution, reducing the possibility of 'detection' while not increasing 'protection' from the abuse, is never questioned.

2 The irony of this, is the apparent frequency of assault in the institutional setting (Musick, 1984).

3 The revelation of the abuse is made only once she has presented some of the course material and children divulge that it has just happened to them.

4 This estimate includes non-contact abuse such as exhibitionism. It excludes the results of numerous individuals for whom there was no information about the age at which their victimization occurred.

5 For ease of reference the female pronoun will be used to refer to the generic child victim and the male pronoun used to refer to the generic adult perpetrator. This usage reflects gender accurately in the majority of cases. This is not to imply that male victims and female perpetrators do not exist.

6 Her parents may also possess this fear, preventing them from reporting the abuse in the event that they know about it (Dickey, 07/87).

7 There are wide individual differences in responses to sexual abuse between children. As such, it will be assumed except where specifically noted that children with developmental disabilities experience a range of symptoms similar to other children.

8 It is not known how this process is confounded in those instances where the child/adolescent has been sterilized. Certainly this could be considered to be shaping the child's sexuality in a "developmentally inappropriate" manner. See Rioux (1979) for a discussion of the psychological effects of sterilization procedures for people with intellectual impairments.

9 Schizophreniform psychoses is a psychotic condition including bizarre behaviour, hallucinations, and delusions.

10 Annotated bibliographies on sexual abuse treatment are available free from the National Clearinghouse on Family Violence.

11 Neither would one want them to.

12 would include group homes, schools, and institutional facilities in which children live in numbers.

13 even when screening has taken place because the offender has no record.

14 Long before intelligence testing occurred, this belief was held, but with the advent of intelligence tests, the testing of convicts became an extremely common procedure. Most of the recent research with regard to the criminal justice system uses IQ scores as the sole criterion for "mental retardation". My concerns with this procedure have been noted elsewhere.

15 Marshall and Barbaree do not work exclusively with offenders with intellectual impairments but have a fair number of "low IQ" offenders in both their assessment and treatment programs.

16 Canadian law expresses these same concerns by defining in the assault legislation what consent is not.

17 This should not be considered a sufficient condition for inability to consent. As it has been shown, many institutionalized adolescent have not had access to sex education and thus would be considered unable to give consent.

18 While the law was archaic and imposed celibacy on women with developmental disabilities for life, adults who exploited adolescents and adults could be caught by its net.

19 If a proposed witness' mental capacity is challenged, this would still be determined at a voir dire hearing.

20 There would be no point discussing the credibility of the testimony of children with intellectual impairments as long as all children are believed to be unable to give credible testimony.

21 It must be remembered that what seemed central for the child might be quite different from what an adult would consider central, e.g., a description of the perpetrator.

22 Such a question would be, "Can you tell me if it happened before your birthday or after your birthday?"

23 Many people are concerned that the rights of the alleged perpetrator will be, abridged by the use of videotapes and the defendant's removal from the courtroom. These are legal questions which must be addressed.

24 would include group homes, schools, and institutional facilities in which children live in numbers.

Recent Publications from The G. Allan Roeher Institute

entourage is a quarterly bilingual magazine that looks at how people with mental handicaps can be supported *by* the community to live, learn, work, and have fun *in* the community. **entourage** includes the most current information on issues and upcoming events, and provides the most comprehensive way of keeping in touch with what's happening in the lives of individuals with a mental handicap.

Subscription: $16 Canadian $18 foreign (1 year)
$30 Canadian $34 foreign (2 years)

Hugs All Around! How Nicholas McCullough Came Home. 1989.

The Pursuit of Leisure: Enriching Lives with People who have a Disability (2nd edition), 1989.
$12.50

Income Insecurity: The Disability Income System in Canada, 1988.
$12.50

The Language of Pain: Perspectives on Behaviour Management, 1988.
$14.95

Keith Edward's Different Day, Karin Melberg Schwier, 1988.
$4.95

Starcross: Out of the Mainstream, John P. Radford and Allison Tipper, 1988.
$12.50

Service Brokerage: Individual Empowerment and Social Service Accountability, Brian Salisbury, Jo Dickey, Cameron Crawford, 1987.
$16.00

Community Living 2000 (Canadian Association for Community Living), 1987.
$2.00

More Education/Integration, 1987.
$15.00

The Family Book: For Parents who have learned that their child has a mental handicap, 1986.
$6.00

Making a Difference: What communities can do to prevent mental handicap and promote lives of quality (NIMR), 1986. Five volumes.
$5.00 each/$20.00 for five.

Prices are subject to change without notice.

ORDER ADDRESS: The G. Allan Roeher Institute
         Kinsmen Building, York University
         4700 Keele Street
         Downsview Ontario
         M3J 1P3
         Telephone: (416) 661-9611